AF326515

SUPERCREATIVITY

SUPERCREATIVITY

Accelerating Innovation in the
Age of Artificial Intelligence

JAMES TAYLOR

Sirmione Publishing is an imprint of P3 Music Limited.
P3 Music Ltd, Stannergate House, 41 Dundee Road West, Dundee DD5 1BN, United Kingdom.

A CIP catalogue record for this book is available from the British Library and the Library of Congress.

ISBN: 978-1-918463-00-2 (Hardcover)
978-1-918463-01-9 (Paperback)
978-1-918463-02-6 (eBook)

Ordering Information

If you would like to share *SuperCreativity* with your team, clients, or event attendees, special discounts are available for bulk purchases of 10 or more.
Many organisations order copies for workshops, conferences, and leadership programmes to spark innovation and inspire creative thinking.
For details on quantity orders or customised bundles, please contact enquiries@jamestaylor.me

Bonus Content

This copy of *SuperCreativity* entitles you to exclusive bonus materials, including worksheets, videos, and additional resources.
To access your bonus content, simply visit www.supercreativitybook.com

Cover design: Scott Witham
Copy editing: Barry Lyons

First Edition, March 2026
Printed on demand in the country where this book was purchased.

*For Alison, my most trusted
creative collaborator.*

ABOUT THE AUTHOR

James Taylor M.B.A., F.R.S.A. began his career managing high-profile rock stars and is now an in-demand keynote speaker, boardroom adviser, and internationally recognised authority on creativity, innovation, and artificial intelligence. For over 20 years, he has advised C-suite executives, entrepreneurs, educators, governments, and business leaders from Silicon Valley to Shanghai on how to design innovative organisations, unlock creative potential, and build a sustainable future.

As host of the *SuperCreativity* podcast and multiple global summits, Taylor has interviewed more than 750 thought leaders, technologists, and authors shaping the future of creativity and technology. His keynotes, workshops, and courses have reached audiences in more than 120 countries, offering insights into how humans and machines can collaborate to solve complex challenges.

His clients include Fortune Global 500 companies, government policymakers, and leading industry associations. Organisations across sectors such as technology, finance, healthcare, energy, and manufacturing bring him in to inspire and educate through his thought-provoking keynotes and interactive workshops.

A Fellow of the Royal Society of the Arts (F.R.S.A.), Taylor divides his time between Hampstead in London, Perthshire in Scotland, and Le Marche in Italy when not speaking on stages worldwide.

CONTENTS

INTRODUCTION

THE SUPERCREATIVE AGE

SuperCreativity (noun)
su·per·cre·a·tiv·i·ty | \ ˌsü-pər-ˌkrē-ˌā-ˈti-və-tē \
"The augmentation of an individual's creative abilities through collaboration with other humans or machines."

A Night at the Royal Albert Hall

The lights went up. The crowd roared. And for nearly three hours, 5,000 people were swept into a musical journey.

It was October 25th, 2009, and I was more than a decade into my career managing the lives and tours of high-profile rock stars. That night, one of my artists was performing at London's legendary Royal Albert Hall. It was a special performance. But what made it transformative was not just the music – it was the decision I made backstage that evening. A decision that would ultimately lead to the book you now hold in your hands.

If you've ever attended a concert, a conference, a play, or a major sporting event, you've likely felt it: that electric moment when a performer, a CEO, or an athlete creates something magical. A song. A character. A speech. A moment that transcends the ordinary.

As a talent manager – and later as a keynote speaker – I've stood at the side of the stage for over three thousand shows. It's a fascinating vantage point. When I look straight ahead, I see the singer under the spotlight, captivating the audience. Look left, and I see the crowd – thousands caught up in the experience. But it's when I glance to my right, or behind me, then I see the full picture.

The Backstage Truth About Creativity

Backstage is where the real magic begins. The lighting crew. The advisors. The musicians. The managers. Sometimes a hundred or more people working in perfect synchronicity to produce what appears on stage as effortless brilliance.

The media loves the myth of the lone genius. The charismatic singer bathed in spotlight. The CEO gracing the front cover of *Forbes*, as if they built the company entirely on their own.

But here's the truth: creativity is not a solo act. Creativity is collaborative. It's a team sport.

Behind every standout moment – on a stage, on a sports field, or in a product launch – there is a network of backstage heroes. Creative collaborators who take a bold idea and help bring it to life.

As I stood in the wings that night at the Royal Albert Hall, I made a pivotal decision. I would step away from managing a few Grammy Award–winning artists to dedicate my life to helping more people – leaders, teams, and professionals – unlock their own creative potential. Whether it's a CEO driving innovation, a manager navigating the impact of AI, or a rising talent looking to do more meaningful work, they all need to tap into deeper creative collaboration to thrive.

The Creativity Crisis

At its core, that's what this book is about: how each of us can unleash our full creative potential – through better collaboration.

But collaboration today takes many forms. It might mean working more closely with teammates, business partners, customers, or suppliers. Increasingly, though, creativity means collaborating with machines – using tools like artificial intelligence to go beyond what humans can do alone.

Today, business is changing at the speed of light. Exponential technologies such as AI, robotics, and quantum computing are reshaping industries and creating disruptive business models almost overnight. Leaders around the world – from San Francisco to Singapore – are searching for insights on how to adapt, stay relevant, and lead through these transformations.

In this new age – where McKinsey predicts that 45% of jobs may be automated over the next two decades – there is one distinctly human competitive advantage that machines can't totally replicate: your creativity.

And don't just take it from me. According to the World Economic Forum's survey of over 1,000 global business leaders, creativity is the number one skill rising most in importance. Why? Because machines will take over the mundane, bureaucratic, and repetitive tasks – leaving creative problem-solving and human ingenuity as our superpowers.

LinkedIn's recent Future of Skills Report echoes the same message. Creativity ranks in the top three most in-demand soft skills, just behind adaptability and resilience. Employers everywhere are under pressure to innovate, differentiate, and stay ahead in a fast-changing, AI-powered economy.

Here's the paradox: just as creativity becomes more valuable than ever, fewer people believe they possess it.

Despite being more connected, educated, and resourced than any generation in history, millions of people feel disconnected from their own creative potential. According to a global Adobe study, only one in three people believe they are creative – even though creativity is consistently ranked as essential to success. Think about that. The majority of people in your company, your community, your country do not believe they possess the very skill most needed in this age of intelligent machines.

Time magazine calls it "The Creativity Crisis". This book is my answer to that crisis.

But before we go further, let's clarify something. You don't need to be a musician, actor, or artist to be creative. If you've ever solved a tricky problem, pitched a new idea, navigated a crisis, or helped others see something in a new way, you've been creative.

Creativity is about bringing new ideas to the mind. Innovation is about bringing new ideas to the world. But without creativity, there is no innovation. Creativity is the engine that drives innovation – whether in the form of new products, services, strategies, or experiences.

But in this new era, creativity is evolving again.

In a world where machines can write, analyse, compose, and code – what does it even mean to be creative today? And more importantly, how can collaborating with artificial intelligence *and* other humans help you unlock your own creative potential?

These are the questions that guide my work today as a keynote speaker and advisor on creativity, innovation, and AI to many of the companies in the *Fortune* Global 500.

That's where the idea of **SuperCreativity** comes in.

What is SuperCreativity?

SuperCreativity is the ability to augment your creativity by collaborating with others – both humans and machines. It's not about human *versus* machine. It's about humans *plus* machines. It's a mindset, a skill set, and increasingly a competitive advantage.

As you'll discover, SuperCreativity isn't the exclusive domain of lone creative geniuses. The good news is that it can be learned – even by individuals and teams who don't see themselves as naturally creative.

SuperCreativity is a methodology I've been teaching to leaders and teams around the world. More and more, individuals and organizations are seeking breakthroughs in their work – and SuperCreativity offers a framework to achieve them.

In this book, you'll discover a new model for twenty-first-century creativity – structured around **three core perspectives** and powered by **eight principles** I call the Eight Ps of *SuperCreativity*. Alongside these, you'll find a powerful set of tools you can apply in your own work.

Human Creativity → *Purpose, Personality, Practice*
Human+Human Creativity → *People, Process, Place*
Human+Machine Creativity → *Product, Persuasion*

Why This Book, Why Now?

SuperCreativity will show how any reader, leader, or team can unlock greater creative potential and leapfrog the competition – by combining individual ingenuity with the power of collaboration: human-to-human and human-to-machine.

It's about harnessing both human connection and exponential technologies like artificial intelligence to *supercharge* the creative potential we all possess.

By the time you finish reading, you'll know how to:

- Develop your creative thinking skills and apply them to real-world challenges
- Accelerate innovation through more creative and collaborative teams
- Augment your personal and team creativity with AI tools
- Apply SuperCreativity across roles, functions, and industries
- Build a more creative and innovative culture in your organization
- Future-proof your relevance in the age of AI

How to Use This Book

There are a number of ways to use this book. Some readers go through it solo. Others form groups at work and tackle it together as a team. You can read the book straight through, return to specific chapters when needed, or (my preferred approach) treat it like an eight-week course.

Here's how: After reading the Introduction, set aside time each Sunday to read the next chapter (or "week") and then apply the lessons – both individually and with your team – throughout the week.

In each chapter, you'll learn from SuperCreatives who apply these ideas organically, as well as from clients and teams I've taught through workshops and keynotes. The final section contains six of the most popular SuperCreativity tools I use with organisations, plus advanced tactics for applying SuperCreativity in your own life and work.

This copy of *SuperCreativity* also entitles you to exclusive bonus materials, including worksheets, videos, and additional resources. To access your bonus content, simply visit www.supercreativitybook.com

A Word Before We Begin

You may not think of yourself as creative…yet.

Maybe someone once told you that creativity was only for artists, actors, or marketers – or for those in the "creative industries". Maybe you were taught to value logic over imagination, structure over play, or certainty over curiosity.

Let me assure you: you are creative. You always have been.

You just need the right mindset, methodology, and tools to unlock what's already within you.

This isn't just a book about creativity, it's a field guide to becoming a **SuperCreator** – someone who can solve complex problems, generate bold ideas, and thrive in collaboration with both humans and machines.

Ready?

Let's begin.

MEET THE SUPERCREATIVES

"I have no special talents.
I am only passionately curious."
– Albert Einstein

The Moment of Realisation

The concept of SuperCreativity was born in 2017 while speaking on creativity, innovation, and artificial intelligence to audiences around the world – from law firms and consultancies to hospitals and high-tech startups. And in every room, I noticed the same pattern.

A handful of individuals stood out, not because they had better ideas, but because they turned ideas into impact. They weren't just thinkers. They were doers. These were the people launching breakthrough products, solving complex problems, reshaping entire industries. They didn't just imagine the future. They built it.

What set them apart wasn't job title, seniority, or even intelligence. It was their ability to **collaborate creatively**, not just with others on their team, but across disciplines, departments, and increasingly… with machines.

By 2018, I began calling these people **SuperCreatives** – and their approach to work – **SuperCreativity**.

SuperCreativity is the amplification of your creative abilities through intentional collaboration with other humans or with machines.

What SuperCreatives Do Differently

These SuperCreatives weren't confined to the arts or "creative industries". I found them everywhere: across every sector, function, and culture. They understood that creativity today isn't a solo act. It's a social, strategic, and increasingly technological act.

- **Educators** reimagining classrooms through co-creation with students and peers
- **Healthcare teams** combining disciplines to deliver more holistic care
- **Product managers** leading cross-functional sprints that put customers at the centre
- **Marketers** collaborating with writers, designers – and yes, AI – to craft impactful campaigns
- **Musicians** co-composing with global artists and intelligent systems
- **Architects and communities** co-designing inclusive and sustainable spaces
- **Entrepreneurs** building hybrid teams of humans and AI agents to accelerate innovation
- **Lawyers, scientists, and engineers** rethinking legacy systems through bold collaboration
- **Sales leaders** blending storytelling, data, and digital tools to deepen relationships
- **Nonprofit founders** creating social movements powered by networks and imagination

These aren't future visions. These are real people. This is happening now.

What Makes Someone a SuperCreative?

Across all these examples, four core patterns emerged:

- **Curiosity** – They ask better questions and challenge assumptions.
- **Collaboration** – They thrive in diverse teams and tap into collective intelligence.
- **Adaptability** – They embrace new tools and shift their thinking with agility.
- **Bias for Action** – They move fast, test ideas, and build momentum.

They aren't limited by job description. They're defined by mindset.

The Three Types of Modern Creativity

As I studied SuperCreatives in action, three distinct modes of creativity emerged:

- **Human Creativity** – The personal foundation: your mindset, originality, and creative skills
- **Human+Human Creativity** – The collaborative dimension: creating with others across roles, disciplines, and cultures
- **Human+Machine Creativity** – The emerging frontier: collaborating with AI and intelligent tools to amplify ideas

These three modes form the backbone of this book.

To help you strengthen each one, we'll explore the **Eight Ps of SuperCreativity** – the key principles that drive creative performance in individuals and teams.

Each chapter focuses on one principle: what it means, why it matters, and how to apply it in your life and work.

The Eight Ps are:
1. **Purpose**
2. **Personality**
3. **Practice**
4. **People**
5. **Process**
6. **Place**
7. **Product**
8. **Persuasion**

Curiosity is the Catalyst

If there's one trait every SuperCreative shares – regardless of role, industry, or background – it's this: **curiosity**.

Julie Sweet, CEO of Accenture, put it simply: "The new normal is continuous learning. We want people who demonstrate curiosity."

Because if creativity is the engine of innovation, then curiosity is the fuel.

Curiosity means asking better questions. Not just "What happened?" but "Why does it work this way?" and "What if we tried something completely different?"

Later in this book, you'll learn a tool called **Curious Questions**. It's helped lawyers discover new revenue streams, marketers spark bold campaigns, and engineers solve problems that had them stuck for months.

In the age of AI, it won't be your answers that set you apart, it will be your questions.

As Kevin Kelly, founding editor of *Wired*, said: "The future belongs to those who can ask better questions, not just find better answers."

Or as Fei-Fei Li, the Godmother of AI put it: "AI is about machines learning from data, but [it's] also about humans learning to ask better questions."

In a noisy world, your edge is clarity. And clarity starts with curiosity.

Where We're Headed

In the pages that follow, you'll meet more SuperCreatives – surgeons, scientists, strategists – who've used curiosity and collaboration to do their most meaningful work.

But before we dive into the tools and frameworks, we need to dismantle a few lies. Let's begin by challenging the three biggest myths of creativity.

MYTHS & TRUTHS

A Sensory Story from Colombia

Warm, Amazonian chocolate dripped from my fingers. The "choco-therapy" ritual – essentially having your hands ceremonially washed in melted chocolate – was just the beginning of what was quickly becoming a multi-sensory dining experience. It was part fine dining, part performance art, and part what-have-you-gotten-me-into from my dinner companion, David – a 6'5", bearded Coloradan and customer experience expert who clearly hadn't expected his evening to involve edible handwashing. We'd arrived in Bogotá just hours earlier to speak at a business conference, and with a free evening to shake off the jet lag, I'd talked him into joining me for a plant-based tasting menu at Elcielo – one of Colombia's most acclaimed restaurants and the first in the country to earn a Michelin star.

"How are we supposed to eat it?" David asked the waitress.

"For the full experience, Chef suggests that you lick the chocolate off," she said.

"Off our own hands or each other's?" I asked with a wink.

The chef was Juan Manuel Barrientos, 34, an entrepreneurial peace activist, whose Elcielo restaurants have quickly become known for giving traditional Colombian cuisine a creative avant-garde twist in order to stimulate the five senses.

After opening his first restaurant in Medellín, Chef Barrientos had quickly expanded with openings in Miami, Bogota, and Washington DC. The restaurant has acquired a worldwide reputation because of dishes like Bonsai-shaped Yuca bread and "Cafetal", Colombian coffee that is paired with native plants and served in a cloud of liquid nitrogen to mimic the misty mountains of Colombia. As incredible as the front of house experience was, it was the creativity backstage that had compelled me to make this culinary pilgrimage.

For 50 years, Colombia had been in a perpetual civil war as Revolutionary Armed Forces of Colombia (FARC) guerrillas, funded by drug barons, battled with government and paramilitary forces. More than 200,000 Colombians, mostly civilians, had died in the conflict and five million more had been displaced.

When the conflict finally ended in 2016 with the signing of a peace accord, Colombia's people were in dire need of reconciliation. In the town of Medellín, once the heart of the Colombian drug trade, Barrientos, then twenty-one-years old, decided to offer cooking courses and employment to wounded combatants and veterans.

Thirteen years later, and a few steps away from where David and I were enjoying this gourmet meal, was a powerful example of creative collaboration and reconciliation.

Behind the scenes in the kitchen former government soldiers like Ruben Dario Romero, who had lost an eye and part of his leg to a land mine, were preparing elaborate dishes alongside Maria, a one-time guerilla in the FARC, the same group responsible to placing the land mine that had nearly ended Ruben's life. Only a few years before, these two wounded warriors would have been on opposite sides of a violent conflict, each seeing the other as the enemy. Now they were cooking and creating Michelin-starred food together.

But what stayed with me wasn't just the edible handwashing. It was what I saw in the kitchen: former competitors and combatants who had become collaborators and co-creators in something world-class and extraordinary. It was a vivid reminder that true creativity rarely happens in isolation. It's born through collaboration – often between those who never imagined they were creative to begin with. What I observed in Elcielo challenged the three most common myths about creativity which hold each of us back from doing our most creative, and therefore our most innovative work.

MYTH No. 1: The Lone Creative Genius

The mainstream media loves to perpetuate what I call the myth of the "lone creative genius". The deification of the billionaire tech CEO (as if they had single handedly created that business) is a useful fiction but it paints out the contribution of others. For every sage on the stage there are hundreds of guides on the side.

Take a moment now to look around you. Maybe you're sitting at your desk, or in a coffee shop, or on a plane. Nearly everything around you started as a kernel of an idea in someone's head before a creative act made it into the product or service you see in front of you. It doesn't matter if it's the book in your hand, the clothes you are wearing, the seat you're sitting in, the art on the walls, the app on your phone, or the laws and legislation that rule your life, all of them were created by men, women or machines. But here's the thing they don't tell you in the movies.

When we think a successful product, service, or company we usually think of one person. Steve Jobs and the iPhone, Sara Blakely and Spanx. But this is just lazy storytelling perpetuated by the media and publicists. The truth is that to really understand how creativity and innovation work, how something goes from being a vague idea to a blockbuster hit, we need to look backstage and understand the role of collaboration in the creative process itself. The messy middle of innovation.

The myth of the "lone creative genius" can be traced back to a sixteenth-century painter and writer named Giorgio Vasari, who penned one of the earliest biographies of artists, *Lives of the Artists*. In it, he painted figures like Leonardo da Vinci and Michelangelo as solitary, divine vessels of inspiration – superhuman talents whose genius seemed to spring from nowhere.

Before Vasari's book, creativity was viewed quite differently. Ancient cultures believed that inspiration flowed through us, not from us. The Greeks credited the Muses. The Romans spoke of a *genius loci*, a kind of spirit of place that imbued environments with creative energy. Creativity was seen as collective, contextual, and often spiritual – something influenced by our surroundings, our mentors, our communities, and the divine.

Vasari flipped that script. His book helped popularize the idea that genius resided within the individual – exclusively and heroically. He famously referred to Michelangelo as "the Divine Michelangelo", casting him as a solitary master, touched by something higher than ordinary mortals.

But the historical record tells a different story.

Michelangelo, like most great artists of his time, worked with a team. We have receipts, contracts, and correspondence that show he hired a small army of skilled assistants to help design, sculpt, and paint many of his most celebrated works – including the ceiling of the Sistine Chapel. He wasn't a lone genius. He was more like a modern film director: providing the vision, guiding the execution, and drawing on the collective skill of a talented crew.

In other words, the myth of the lone genius wasn't fact. It was Renaissance-era PR.

Vasari edited out the collaborators to make the genius shine brighter. He erased the team to elevate the hero.

And we've been buying into that narrative ever since.

But it's time to let go of it.

Creativity doesn't happen in a vacuum. It happens in relationships – in the friction of opposing ideas, in the energy of collaboration, in the messy, beautiful complexity of people working together toward something bold and new.

Don't fall for the lone genius myth. It's a fiction dressed as history.

The truth is far more empowering: you don't have to be a genius to do something genius. You just have to be willing to create, contribute, and collaborate.

MYTH No. 2: The Creative Type

Once Vasari's idea of the "lone creative genius" had taken root it was only a matter of time before the myth of "the creative type" would take hold. Over the subsequent centuries, and then compounded during the Enlightenment period that glorified "the great man", the false narrative of the creative type became received wisdom.

The myth of the creative type says that there are creative people and there are uncreative people. Nothing could be further from the truth. Indeed modern science has shown us that all of us are born with almost unlimited creative potential. What is important is what we choose to do with it.

In the 1960s, NASA developed a test to measure creativity in engineers. Dr. George Land's study found that 98% of four- to five-year-olds scored with high levels of creativity. This dropped to 30% by the time they were 10, and when someone reached adulthood their creativity levels had plummeted to as low as two percent.

Today, in my role as a keynote speaker on the topics of creativity, innovation, and artificial intelligence, I get to travel around the world inspiring, educating, and entertaining audiences. A common question I sometimes ask on stage is to see a show of hands from those people who consider themselves to be creative or good creative thinkers. If I'm speaking to tech CEOs in San Francisco around half of the audience will raise their hands but if my audience consists of lawyers in London or marketers in Manila only around a third will raise their hands.

There are two main reasons why people don't consider themselves to be creative. The first is because frankly their creativity has been metaphorically beaten out of them by an educational system that favours rote learning and facts over flexibility of thinking. But often the second reason is that they hold the mistaken belief that some people are born creative while others aren't.

A much better way of thinking about creativity is on a continuum from Small C creativity on one side to Big C creativity on the other. Small C creativity is when we do those things which are new, novel and useful. Big C creativity is when you do work which is new, novel, useful *and* changes the domain, field or industry in which you work.

For example, a few years ago I was in Beijing and visited a restaurant where I was served the spiciest soup I have ever tasted. Once I had drunk a gallon of ice water and got my breath back, I asked the staff what was in the soup. They introduced me to Szechuan peppercorns and before I returned home, I bought a small bag of the small cannonball-shaped explosive devices. A few weeks later I was enjoying a holiday in Italy and had taken a few of these peppercorns with me. That evening I set about making a dish of penne arrabbiata, a simple Italian meal of penne pasta, olive oil, garlic, tomatoes, and chilli. However, instead of using the usual traditional chilli peppers I threw in a few of the crushed Szechuan peppercorns. The final result was a pasta dish that increased your internal temperature and heart rate and would have no doubt drawn the scorn of my Italian neighbours. My version of "penne arrabbiata" with Italian tomatoes and pasta combined with Chinese peppers was new, novel and useful. However it is unlikely to ever change the world of the culinary arts. For that we need to move further along the continuum to creating something that is new, novel, useful *and* changes a niche, field, industry, or domain.

An example of someone doing Big C creative work was Zaha Hadid, an Iraqi-born, London-trained architect known as the "Queen of the Curve". Zaha's buildings epitomised her love of experimentation, spatial compositions, and the testing of new materials, technologies, and construction techniques. When I lived in Dubai, I would walk past one of her buildings, The Opus by OMNIYAT, almost every day and marvel at how Zaha and her team were able to create these large solid buildings look like they were fluid and opaque.

Marc Kushner, founder of architectural website Architizer summed up the feelings of many within his profession by saying that Zaha Hadid "is amongst a handful of architects that truly transformed the field within my lifetime. In doing so, she became as well-known for her buildings. To the world, she was Zaha."

Doing something which is new, novel and useful is necessary but not sufficient for creating work which is "Big C". For that one needs to create something which also changes a niche, field, industry or domain.

Zaha Hadid is an example of someone whose work reaches what could be defined as "Big C", but every industry, field, or domain has them. Warren Buffett changed the world of investing, Steve Jobs changed the technology industry, Frida Kahlo changed the world of art, JK Rowling changed children's literature. And perhaps the height of this is those who don't just change a domain but create entirely new ones. For this we can think of Aristotle for physics, Wilhelm Wundt for psychology, or Charles Hull for 3D printing.

So as you can see there is no such thing as "the creative type". Creativity is not passed on like hair colour or eye colour. There is no creativity gene. We are all born with almost unlimited creative potential. A much better way of thinking of creativity is as a continuum and our job is to push ourselves to doing the kind of Big C creative work that changes the world.

Creativity is not a fixed trait. It's a muscle. And like any muscle, it grows through use.

You weren't born knowing how to speak, write, code, lead, or negotiate. You learned.

Creativity works the same way. With the right tools, mindset, and practice, anyone can strengthen it.

MYTH No. 3: Creativity Is Magic

Today Singapore is one of the most successful, prosperous, global, and innovative small countries in the world. This small city state has GDP per capita of over USD $87,000, ranking it among the highest in the world. Singapore was recently ranked in fourth place in the annual Global Innovation Index (GII) while also retaining the top spot in Asia as a whole. Few would have imagined that when the country won its independence from the UK in 1958 that it would go on to be celebrated as one of the most creative and innovative city states.

So how did a country go from being one of the poorest in Asia to having higher GDP per capita than the USA, Sweden, or the UK? The answer lies in the skills that its founding father Lee Kuan Yew set about developing in his people. Lee recognised that Singapore didn't have the natural resources of nearby Malaysia or Thailand so he chose to invest in another type of resource, his people. Indeed he once said, "The human mind must be creative, must be self-generating." Over the coming decades Singapore set about teaching creative thinking skills in its schools, universities, businesses and government ministries. As a result it went on to become one of the most creative and innovative countries in the world.

The idea that creativity and creative thinking are skills can be taught and developed in an individual and a people is now widely understood with study after study backing up ways in which to nurture this skill. Much like learning a language, creativity and creative thinking is something we can improve over time. Indeed in the 1960s Ellis Paul Torrance and his team of researchers at the University of Minnesota built upon the work of J.P. Guilford to devise "The Torrance Test" to measure someone's creative thinking abilities. This test, based upon measuring your divergent and convergent thinking skills, is scored on four scales: fluency (the total number of ideas generated in response to a stimulus), flexibility (the number of different categories of relevant responses), originality (the statistical rarity of the responses), and elaboration (the amount of detail in the responses).

When I deliver creative thinking workshops I train business executives, government officials, engineers, educators, and even school children on a simple set of creative thinking tools to develop their creativity. I've had the joy of delivering these workshops in Mexico City, Singapore, Ho Chi Minh City, Marrakesh, and Berlin, and if I were to measure someone's creativity before the workshop and then after the workshop, I would see it increase. This idea of creativity being a teachable and trainable skill, much like learning a language, is often seen as an anathema to those who view creativity as something akin to magic.

Books like Elizabeth Gilbert's *The Big Magic* and Julia Cameron's *The Artist's Way* write about creativity in mystical tones. While I enjoy their writing and agree with them about many aspects of creativity, I also believe there is a danger in wrapping creative work in a cloak of mysticism and "woo-woo". Creativity is not magic. Creativity is like magic. Creativity can be a taught and developed in an empirical, measurable and scientific way. As the writer Arthur C. Clarke once said, "Any sufficiently advanced technology is indistinguishable from magic." When we watch a great movie or listen to a powerful piece of music or use exponential technology like AI, it can feel like magic but in truth it originated from thousands of creative minds collaborating together.

Great ideas don't appear out of nowhere. They grow. They evolve. They're sparked by patterns, shaped by feedback, and built through process.

Let's go back to Elcielo. That surreal dinner wasn't the product of spontaneous brilliance. It was the result of **years** of testing, iteration, and collaboration – between chefs, suppliers, designers, and customers.

What felt magical was actually engineered. Refined. Structured.

Creativity might *feel* magical. But it's not magic. It's method.

That's good news. Because if it's a process, it's something you can learn. You don't need to wait for inspiration. You can use tools and build systems that spark it.

Later in this book I will teach you some of these tools and systems which are proven to increase both your own creativity and that of your team. But more on that later…

Three Truths to Remember

Let's replace those myths with something more powerful – truths you can build on.

1. Creativity is not a talent.

It's a skill, a mindset, and a set of habits. You weren't born uncreative. You may have just stopped practicing.

2. Creativity is not only a solo act.

It thrives in collaboration – with people, with teams, and increasingly, with intelligent machines.

3. Creativity is not magic.

It follows patterns and processes. It can be taught, refined, and scaled.

In the chapters ahead, you'll meet people – surgeons, designers, entrepreneurs, engineers – who are applying these truths to do remarkable things. And in the process have become Super-Creative.

- You'll learn how to develop your own creative muscle.
- How to collaborate better with people and with machines.
- How to build habits that spark insight and drive innovation.

But before we do that, we need to start at the centre of all creative work.

Not with skills. Not with strategies.

But with something deeper.

We begin with **Purpose**.

PART 1

HUMAN CREATIVITY

"To create is to live twice." – Albert Camus

What Is Human Creativity?

It begins with a handprint.

Somewhere in northern Spain, pressed onto the wall of a cave over 40,000 years ago, a human being placed their palm against the stone and blew ochre pigment across their fingers. The result was a red outline – a ghostly signature. They weren't doing it for fame or profit. They were saying: I was here. This is me.

Long before we built businesses or designed technology, we created. Creativity wasn't decoration – it was survival. Our ancestors fashioned tools from flint, wove fibres into nets, painted animals in torch-lit caves, and passed on knowledge through songs and stories. Evolutionary biologists point to this as a major leap in human development: the moment when *Homo sapiens* stopped merely reacting to the environment and began reshaping it.

The Power of Original Thought

The expansion of the prefrontal cortex – responsible for abstract thought, problem-solving, and forward planning – gave us the unique ability to imagine scenarios that didn't yet exist. This capacity to mentally simulate possible futures was a game-changer. It allowed early humans to devise strategies for hunting, innovating, collaborating – and, over time, for building complex social and economic systems.

Anthropologists have shown that early forms of creative expression – like symbolic art, ritual, and storytelling – played a key role in group cohesion. In other words, creativity was not just personal – it was social. It allowed us to communicate values, share knowledge, and align around shared goals. The first stories weren't entertainment; they were leadership tools.

The Twenty-First Century Creative Challenge

The same capacity that helped early humans out-think predators and outlast ice ages is now what helps companies navigate disruption, imagine new markets, and reinvent how they deliver value. Today, creativity continues to serve the same fundamental purpose – but now within boardrooms, business plans, and product roadmaps. Whether you're designing a new service, navigating market disruption, or rethinking a customer journey, creativity remains one of your most valuable – and distinctively human – skills.

And yet, in many professional environments, creativity is still treated as a "nice to have" rather than a strategic imperative. It's often siloed in marketing departments or relegated to brainstorming sessions. But in a world defined by volatility, complexity, and rapid technological change, creativity is no longer optional. It's how we solve problems, adapt, and grow.

Why Human Creativity Still Matters

It's also, as you've now learned, measurable. Psychologist Mihaly Csikszentmihalyi, who pioneered research on the "flow state", spent decades studying creativity – not as some mystical force, but as a set of identifiable traits, processes, and practices. He argued that creativity arises when individuals engage in challenging tasks that require skill, autonomy, and full immersion. We now know that creativity can be cultivated, trained, and scaled across teams and organisations. It's a meta-skill: a force multiplier that enables innovation, resilience, and long-term value creation.

How This Part Works

But before we can build that skill set, we need to start with something more foundational. What is the purpose of your creative work? What motivates you to innovate, adapt, and express new ideas? In this section, we'll explore the three internal drivers of creativity – Purpose, Personality, and Practice – and how they set the stage for creative work at every level.

That journey begins with the first of our three core elements to human creativity: purpose – the deeper "why" behind everything you create.

CHAPTER 1

PURPOSE (WHY WE CREATE)

"We don't stop playing because we grow old; we grow old because we stop playing." – George Bernard Shaw

The Old Man and the Cake

I was five years old, dressed in a miniature sailor outfit that looked like something from a costume shop. In my small hands, I clutched a birthday cake almost as wide as I was tall. The stage lights at the Paul Mason Vineyard amphitheatre near San Francisco were blinding. Beyond them, I could just make out the outlines of thousands of people in the audience – a sea of shadows and excited murmurs.

My job was simple: walk across the stage and present the cake to the man at the piano.

That man, I would learn many years later, was Oscar Peterson – widely regarded as one of the greatest jazz pianists of the twentieth century. At the time, I didn't know who he was. I just knew he seemed kind and very old, and that I was nervous and eager to get backstage again where my new Millennium Falcon Star Wars toy was waiting.

He smiled as I handed him the cake. The crowd applauded, and I turned and walked off, my part in the evening complete. What I didn't see – but would come to understand years later

– was the transformation that took place the moment his hands touched the keys.

Oscar wasn't the only magician on stage that night. Also performing was the legendary French violinist Stéphane Grappelli. I remember him well – not just for his music, but for the quiet contrast he presented before and after each performance. Offstage, he moved slowly, gingerly. He was in his early 70s by then, with the slightly stooped posture of someone who'd spent years carrying a violin case and perhaps a few more carrying the weight of time itself.

But then the lights would go up.

And something extraordinary would happen.

He'd lift the violin to his chin, and with the first note, he transformed. The years seemed to roll off him like a heavy coat shrugged from his shoulders. His fingers danced. His posture straightened. His eyes lit up with mischief and joy. It wasn't just technical precision – it was a kind of resurrection. He didn't just play. He became.

That was the first time I understood something essential about creativity. It's not only about making something. It's about becoming something. It's about reconnecting with the most vital part of ourselves. For Stéphane, performing wasn't a job – it was a portal. It took him back to youth, to joy, to meaning.

That, I realised, is one of the fundamental reasons we create – to play. To tap into that feeling of aliveness. To shed the years, the titles, the baggage, and return to the simple joy of doing something for the sheer wonder of it.

But as we grow older, so does our creative purpose. What begins in play evolves – into self-expression, into ambition, and sometimes into legacy.

The Three Drives of Purposeful Creativity

Over the years, in conversations with clients ranging from CEOs and HR directors to musicians and software engineers, I've noticed a pattern. Our creative drive tends to evolve across three overlapping motivations:

1. **Creativity as Play** – The instinctive joy of creating for its own sake.
2. **Creativity as Self-Expression** – The urge to say something meaningful, to be seen and heard.
3. **Creativity as Legacy** – The desire to leave something that outlives us.

These aren't stages to tick off like items on a career ladder. They don't come with a fixed order or a clear end. They rise and fall, blend and blur. You might start writing a novel out of pure play, discover it carries your deepest beliefs, and ultimately hope it resonates long after you're gone.

Each of these drivers offers something different – but together they form the emotional fuel of our most meaningful work.

Let's take a closer look at each.

Purpose No. 1: Creativity as Play

I grew up in the 1980s, which meant my early creative toolkit consisted of Play-Doh, LEGO, and the maddening magic of Etch A Sketch (shake once and your Sesame Street drawing was gone forever). I wasn't building anything impressive. I was building dinosaurs with two heads, castles with no doors, and whatever Play-Doh monstrosity I could mash into the carpet before my parents noticed. But that was the point. Watch any child deep in the act of painting, stacking blocks, or inventing a game with absolutely no rules, and you'll see true creative flow. No fear of failure. No obsession with outcomes. Just pure, curious, joyful making.

We're all born with that instinct, but for too many of us this propensity for child-like (not childish) curiosity and creativity has left us.

What happened?

School happened. Rules happened. Standardised testing happened. Then came offices, deadlines, and quarterly KPIs. Somewhere along the line, play got traded for productivity.

But here's the secret: play isn't frivolous. It's foundational.

Play is where imagination meets experimentation. It's where ideas collide in unexpected ways. Many of the most impactful innovations in business and technology didn't begin as fully-formed ideas. They began as experiments. As curiosities. As a scientist, an engineer or an entrepreneur asking herself or others, "Imagine if..."

Google's famous "20% time" – where employees could use part of their workweek to explore passion projects – led to the creation of Gmail, Google Maps, and AdSense. Pixar encourages playful storyboarding long before a script is locked in. IDEO builds creative play into its design thinking process for companies like Ford, Moderna, H&M, and Procter & Gamble. Playfulness isn't opposed to seriousness – it's how seriousness often begins.

When creative work feels empty or purely transactional, motivation fades. Neuroscience and organizational psychology both confirm this. In her research at Harvard, Teresa Amabile found that people are most creative when they believe their work has purpose. In fact, progress toward meaningful goals – not recognition or rewards – is what fuels deep creative engagement.

Even in my own work, some of my best keynote ideas or creativity frameworks didn't arrive when I was sitting at my desk. They showed up when I was walking in the hills, playing with metaphors, having conversations at conferences, or sketching mind maps on a napkin on a long-haul flight.

Creativity starts in play. The trick is to protect that space – especially as we grow older and the stakes feel higher.

Purpose No. 2: Creativity as Self-Expression

Eventually, play becomes something more. You don't just want to make – you want to say something. To articulate a point of view. To put your fingerprint on the world.

In the 1970s, Yvon Chouinard was a climber and self-taught blacksmith who began crafting his own climbing gear – not to start a business, but to protect the rock faces he loved from damage caused by conventional equipment. That act of personal purpose sparked what would become Patagonia, one of the world's most admired outdoor brands. Chouinard's mission was never just about selling jackets; it was about preserving the natural world. That deeper "why" shaped every creative decision the company made – from pioneering recycled materials and launching the Worn Wear repair program, to placing provocative ads like "Don't Buy This Jacket" to challenge overconsumption. In 2022, Chouinard went a step further, transferring ownership of Patagonia to a trust and nonprofit so that all profits could be used to combat climate change. His story is a powerful example of how purpose-driven creativity can build not only enduring products, but a movement – and how a single founder's values can scale into global innovation.

This is where creativity becomes a vehicle for identity.

When I started building my speaking business, I didn't just want to speak or consult. I wanted to advocate for something: that creativity is a superpower in the age of AI. That we are not being replaced by machines – we are being called to collaborate with them in more imaginative ways.

That shift – from making to meaning – is where self-expression lives.

I see it all the time in founders of companies and countries. They don't just want to build a product or nation. They want to build something that represents their values. That reflects the world as they think it should be.

I once worked with a designer who created a clothing brand rooted in sustainability and local craftsmanship. When I asked her why she started it, she said: "Because I was tired of how fast fashion treats people and the planet. I wanted to show another way." That's self-expression in its most purposeful form.

Michael Gerber, in *The E-Myth*, famously said that every entrepreneur is three people in one: the technician, the manager, and the visionary. But in my experience, it's the visionary – the one creating from conviction – who drives the kind of work that lasts.

And here's the truth: you don't need a canvas or a startup to express yourself.

You express yourself every time you pitch a bold idea in a meeting, write an email that persuades, design a process that serves people better, or lead in a way that reflects your values – not just your KPIs.

Because self-expression, at its core, is not about being loud. It's about being clear. It's how purpose becomes visible. It's how your inner "why" shows up in the outer world.

Creativity becomes leadership when your ideas align with your intent – and your intent aligns with what matters.

Purpose No. 3: Creativity as Legacy

And then there's the long view.

You reach a point – sometimes after a loss, sometimes after a success – when you look at your work and ask: Will any of this last? Will it matter to anyone else when I'm no longer here to explain it?

That's when creativity becomes about legacy.

Legacy isn't always grand. It doesn't have to be your name on a building or a bestselling book. It can be the culture you nurtured in your company. The mentees you encouraged when they were still finding their voice. The systems you designed that made work a little more human.

A few years ago, I spoke with a retired tech executive who had overseen billion-dollar product launches. But when I asked what he was most proud of, he said: "That people still call to ask for advice. That they trust I'll help, even when I have nothing to gain."

Legacy is quiet like that. Often invisible. But incredibly powerful.

For some, legacy comes through creative output. For others, through the values they embody. Either way, legacy is where purpose intersects with time. It's the long shadow your work casts across the future.

As the poet Shelley wrote, "The music lives after the instrument is destroyed."

Why Purpose Matters More Than Ever

We now operate in a world of increasingly intelligent tools. Artificial intelligence can generate reports, design interfaces, write marketing copy, and even compose original music. In many cases, it can replicate human creativity with speed, scale, and accuracy that surpasses the average professional.

But it can't do this: care.

It doesn't care why a line matters, why a story resonates, why an experience delights. It doesn't feel urgency, or joy, or regret. It doesn't know what it means to be human.

Purpose is what separates human creativity from machine output.

Purpose is what makes you keep going when the draft is a mess, the funding hasn't come, or no one applauds at the end of the talk. Purpose is what connects your work to others – because people don't just want what you've made. They want to know why you made it.

That's why this chapter comes before personality or process. Because without a clear why, the rest is performance. Style over substance. Efficiency without direction.

So let me ask you:

Why do you create?

- What brings you alive when you work?
- What problem do you feel called to solve?
- And what do you hope will remain – after the lights go down, after the last word is spoken?

Because when you know your purpose, your work stops being just activity. It becomes a contribution.

And that, in the end, is the most creative act of all.

Purpose is the compass. It gives your creativity direction.

But direction alone isn't enough.

Because how you bring ideas to life – how you think, explore, decide, and deliver – isn't shaped by purpose alone.

It's shaped by you.

Your temperament. Your timing. Your working style. Your appetite for risk.

Your rhythm of focus and flow. Your weird rituals that no one else understands but somehow help you get in the zone.

These things aren't quirks. They're clues.

Because creativity isn't one-size-fits-all. It's fingerprinted.

So now you know your why. That's your anchor. Your fuel.

But next, we need to explore how you create: what drives your style, your strengths, and your flow.

That's where we go next:

Personality.

Next Actions

Write Your Creative Purpose Statement

In one bold paragraph (or a single, unforgettable sentence), capture why you create. What fuels your fire? What change do you want your work to make in the world?

1. **Reframe a Current Project with Purpose**

   Pick one project you're working on right now. Ask yourself: *What's the deeper reason behind this work?* If it feels misaligned, how might you reframe it to bring more meaning and intention to the process?

2. **Protect Time for Play**

   Block off one hour this week for playful, non-outcome–driven creation. No goals, no KPIs – just curiosity. What shows up when the stakes are low but the energy is high?

Download the worksheet for this chapter on Purpose as well as bonus content at www.supercreativitybook.com

Reflect and Reframe

Questions to Ask Yourself

- When was the last time I felt deeply alive in my creative work – and what was I doing?
- What values keep showing up in the ideas, projects, or people I'm drawn to?
- If I had to pass something on – an idea, a way of working, a principle – what would I want it to be?
- What's one small change I could make this week to align my work more closely with my purpose?

Key Takeaways

- **Purpose is fuel.** It gives your creativity direction, energy, and resilience – especially when the work gets hard or the outcome is uncertain.
- **Creativity is not just about making things.** It's about becoming someone. The act of creating shapes who you are and what you stand for.
- **Play is foundational, not frivolous.** It's how many breakthrough ideas begin – in curiosity, joy, and experimentation.
- **Self-expression is how purpose becomes visible.** Every system you build, every message you craft, every decision you make is a chance to show what matters.
- **Legacy doesn't have to be loud.** It can be quiet, human, and lasting. What you create today can ripple far beyond your timeline.

CHAPTER 2

PERSONALITY
(WHAT KIND OF CREATIVE ARE YOU)

"Always be a first-class version of you instead of a second-rate version of somebody else." – Judy Garland

The Two Paths to SuperCreativity (Lightning and Fire)

In the fall of 1924, F. Scott Fitzgerald sat in a rented villa on the French Riviera, putting the final touches on *The Great Gatsby*. He was only 28. The novel had come to him with unusual clarity. He worked intensely, obsessively, sculpting every sentence like marble. The result was one of the most iconic novels in American literature – crafted in a burst of brilliance.

Meanwhile, across the Atlantic, another great writer worked at a very different pace. Mark Twain, already in his forties, took years to refine *Adventures of Huckleberry Finn*. He rewrote entire chapters, wrestled with tone and structure, and discovered the story more than he planned it. His process was less flash of lightning, more slow burn.

Fitzgerald and Twain. Lightning and fire.

One struck fast, with clarity and precision. The other simmered, discovering the shape of his work along the way. Both changed literature. Both created lasting impact. But their paths were wildly different.

We see this contrast everywhere.

Orson Welles was just 25 when he made *Citizen Kane*. A conceptual innovator. The kind who arrives with a vision and remakes the rules.

Alfred Hitchcock, by contrast, took decades to refine his voice. His masterpieces – *Vertigo, Rear Window, Psycho* – came later in life. They were earned through years of iteration, experimentation, failure, and refinement. Fire.

This is one of the great paradoxes of creativity: some ideas arrive like thunderbolts. Others take time. And your path – lightning or fire – is shaped not just by chance, but by personality.

Creative Personalities in Action

You see it in business, too.

Alibaba founder Jack Ma is lightning. He moves fast, breaks things, and has a bias for action. He grew Alibaba from idea to one of the largest e-commerce empires in the world with visionary thinking and bold moves.

Microsoft CEO Satya Nadella is fire. His transformation of Microsoft wasn't a single bold idea. It was a steady series of culture shifts, product refinements, and renewed purpose. His innovation came not through disruption but through evolution.

Both approaches work.

Some people create like entrepreneur Whitney Wolfe Herd – launching online dating platform Bumble in bold strokes and owning a new category. Others are more like James Dyson – meticulously prototyping 5,000 versions of a vacuum cleaner before releasing one that worked.

Some, like songwriters Billie Eilish and Finneas, spend years quietly experimenting in a bedroom studio. Others, like Virgil Abloh, artistic director at Louis Vuitton, explode into the scene with a disruptive remix of culture and form.

Your personality matters. And it's not just about pace. It's about how you think, how you adapt, and how you create.

The SuperCreative Personality

By now, you've hopefully let go of the myth that creativity is some mysterious gift bestowed on the few.

You were born creative. But the way you express that creativity is shaped by something deeper: your personality.

Mihaly Csikszentmihalyi spent decades studying high-performing creatives – painters, scientists, engineers, entrepreneurs. He noticed a common thread. Not a personality type – but a personality complexity.

Creative people often carry contradictions. They're both playful and focused. Imaginative and grounded. Bold and vulnerable.

But one trait stands out: openness to experience.

Openness is a cornerstone of the Big Five personality traits. It shows up as curiosity, imagination, emotional depth, an appreciation of beauty, and a willingness to explore unfamiliar ideas. Studies show it's one of the strongest predictors of creativity – across fields, industries, and cultures.

Still, openness isn't the whole story. In working with SuperCreatives – across industries from fashion to pharma – I've observed a constellation of patterns that keep appearing.

Let's explore a few of them – not as prescriptions, but as mirrors.

10 Patterns of SuperCreatives

These aren't boxes to tick. They're tendencies you may already notice in yourself – or can intentionally develop over time. Don't think of them as fixed traits. Think of them as components of your personality.

1. **Physical Energy**

   SuperCreatives manage their energy like elite athletes. Some rise early, some work in sprints, some nap religiously. But when they're on, they're focused and fully engaged.

2. **Smart Yet Naive**

   They blend knowledge with beginner's mind. They ask questions others are too proud – or too programmed – to ask. Naivety lets them imagine new possibilities. Intelligence helps make them real.

3. **Playful with Discipline**

   They flirt with ideas and follow through with grit. The best creatives know how to finish. Play opens the door. Discipline builds what's behind it.

4. **Imaginative and Grounded**

   They dream big, but they also hit deadlines. Vision matters, but so does execution. Oprah Winfrey isn't just an icon because of her message, she's an empire builder who made it happen.

5. **Introverted and Extroverted**

   Some SuperCreatives go deep in solitude. Others buzz with energy in groups. Most toggle between both – knowing when they need noise, and when they need quiet.

6. **Humble and Proud**

   They credit their teams but stand by their work. Brené Brown calls this "strong back, soft front". Confidence with vulnerability. Clarity with care.

7. **Gender-Fluid Thinking**

   They move beyond binary traits. SuperCreatives don't care whether an idea is "masculine" or "feminine". They borrow from all styles and modes to suit the moment.

8. **Rebellious and Conservative**

   They learn the rules – then break them. Miles Davis mastered bebop before creating cool jazz. Steve Jobs studied calligraphy before designing Apple.

9. **Open and Sensitive**

   They feel the world intensely. That emotional range allows them to notice details, connect ideas, and create work that resonates.

10. **Passionate Yet Objective**

    They care deeply. But they also edit ruthlessly. Passion gets the draft out. Objectivity gets the final cut.

Do you need all ten? No. But the more of them you can cultivate, the more resilient – and potent – your creativity becomes.

So... Which Are You?

Are you lightning or fire? Do you leap or do you simmer?

Do you thrive in solitude – or in collaboration? Do you love starting things – or finishing them?

There's no right answer. The only wrong move is not knowing your own creative personality.

If you're lightning, build systems that capture ideas quickly. Don't wait. Strike, then refine. If you're fire, create routines that support deep work. Don't rush. Let ideas simmer.

Either way, the goal isn't to mimic someone else's process. It's to know your own. It's about being a first-class version of yourself.

The more you understand your creative personality, the better you'll be at choosing the right tools, collaborators, and environments. You'll waste less energy forcing workflows that don't fit. And you'll unlock more flow in the ways that do.

From Personality to Practice

Understanding how you work is powerful. But knowing isn't doing.

The real shift happens when you build practices that match your personality – habits that take your potential and make it consistent, repeatable, and impactful.

Because whether you're lightning or fire, the truth remains: creative breakthroughs don't come from waiting for the muse. They come from showing up. Daily.

In the next chapter, we'll look at how SuperCreatives build rituals and systems that support momentum – not just inspiration.

Let's look at…

Process.

Next Actions

Do This Week
1. **Identify Your Creative Style**
   Are you more lightning or fire? Write it down. Describe how it shows up in your projects, your pace, and your process.
2. **Partner with Your Opposite**
   Think of someone whose creative personality is different from yours. How might a collaboration between you unlock new results neither of you could achieve alone?

Download the worksheet for this chapter on Personality as well as bonus content at www.supercreativitybook.com

Reflect and Reframe

Questions to Ask Yourself
- What kind of creative work energizes me – and what drains me?
- Where does my personality help me create? Where does it get in the way?
- What environments, rhythms, or rituals allow me to do my best work?

Key Takeaways

- Your creative personality shapes how you work, ideate, and collaborate.
- There's no single ideal type. Great creatives span the spectrum.

- Awareness of your personality helps you build better teams, pick better tools, and create with more ease.
- Creativity is fingerprinted. Own your process. Honour your pattern.
- You don't need to change who you are. You need to design *for* who you are.

CHAPTER 3

PRACTICE
(WHAT HABITS DO I NEED TO CREATE)

"You can have many great ideas in your head, but what makes the difference is the action. Without action upon an idea, there will be no manifestation, no results, and no reward." – Miguel Ruiz

Talent Is Only the Price of Admission

Most people assume that great performers are just naturally gifted – that they step onto the stage and effortlessly deliver brilliance. But behind every seemingly effortless performance lies something far less glamorous: relentless, obsessive practice.

Take Nikki Glaser's hosting gig at the 2025 Golden Globes. She didn't just glance over her monologue a few times and hope for the best. She rehearsed it 93 times. That's not a typo. She built two writers" rooms to refine her material. She tested jokes in front of comedy club audiences, tweaking her timing and delivery based on live reactions. She even studied past hosts like Tina Fey and Amy Poehler, analysing what made their performances work.

By the time Glaser walked onto that stage, she wasn't just prepared – she was bulletproof. Every pause, punchline, and pivot had been road-tested and fine-tuned. What appeared effortless was the product of discipline. And like any great performer, she didn't practice alone – she built her performance in partnership with writers, audiences, and trusted collaborators.

And that's the point. You might never host the Golden Globes, but in your world – whether it's launching a product, leading a pitch, or defending a case – the same principle applies: what looks effortless is almost always the result of structured, deliberate practice.

Psychologist Anders Ericsson, who spent decades studying elite performers from violinists to fighter pilots, called this "deliberate practice". It's not about mindlessly repeating a task – it's about practicing with clear goals, immediate feedback, and constant refinement. Glaser didn't just repeat her set; she iterated it. That's the difference between practice that makes you tired and practice that makes you better.

Mastery Is Not Born – It's Built

In business, we see a similar mindset in Microsoft CEO Satya Nadella. Unlike his predecessor Steve Ballmer, who was known for off-the-cuff bravado, Nadella treats every major presentation as a high-stakes performance. Each keynote undergoes multiple iterations.

One of his key practices is to run through his speech in front of different internal audiences, including trusted Microsoft executives and communication specialists. He treats these people as part of his practice system – partners who stress-test his message before the world hears it. Each run-through is followed by a detailed debrief, where he refines his phrasing, removes unnecessary complexity, and ensures his key points resonate. He also places a strong emphasis on visual storytelling, working closely with designers to ensure that his slides or visual aids support his message rather than distract from it.

When Nadella delivered Microsoft's AI strategy at the Build Conference, his words felt natural and his vision compelling. But none of it was spontaneous. His calm, deliberate style was forged through disciplined, behind-the-scenes practice.

This is Ericsson's principle in action: great performers shorten the gap between action and feedback. Nadella doesn't just rehearse – he builds rapid feedback loops into his preparation, so each run is sharper than the last.

Even in smaller internal meetings, Nadella is known for his thoughtful pauses and precise articulation, habits that have been honed through repeated practice. Employees who have observed him speak behind closed doors say he often practices different ways to explain the same concept, ensuring that he can adapt his message to different audiences.

The lesson? Great performers aren't born – they are made through repetition, feedback, and refinement.

From Goals to Practice

The week between Christmas and New Year is one of my favourite times of year. The phone is quiet. The inbox slows. No keynotes or meetings. It's a time for reflection and planning – both for me and for my team.

We start by reviewing the previous 11 months: what worked, what didn't. Then we look ahead – identifying new projects to start and old ones to sunset. And finally, we do something different from most companies: we focus more on creating a practice than on setting goals.

Goal-setting is useful. It gives us direction – the what. But it doesn't provide the how, when, or why. Goals can offer a sugar rush when we set them and a sugar crash when we miss them. Practices, by contrast, are systems that sustain progress.

Let me explain with an example.

Let's say your goal is to lose 10 pounds. Traditional thinking breaks that down into sub-goals – lose two pounds in 30 days by exercising. But studies show that 25% of people give up on their New Year's resolutions within the first month, and only one percent stick with them for a year.

Now imagine instead you built a practice – like walking for an hour after dinner every day. No pressure, no milestones. Just a consistent habit. The result? You'll likely lose the weight without fixating on the outcome. And over time, the habit changes not just your health, but your identity.

Practice in Action: Business Examples

When a tech firm that builds real-time operating systems for the automotive industry brought me in to help their sales leaders, they weren't lacking goals. The VP of sales had set an ambitious target: increase revenue by 30% in 12 months.

Instead of focusing only on targets, I guided the team to develop creative thinking tools and, more importantly, to build new sales practices. Daily pitch reviews. Weekly objection-handling drills. The use of AI tools for monthly reviews of transcripts from sales calls. These routines created continuous feedback loops – small, rapid cycles where performance was measured, reflected on, and improved. These micro-routines were more effective than any vision statement. And just as importantly, they were shared routines – reinforced in team meetings, peer reviews, and informal check-ins. Practice multiplied because it was embedded in relationships.

Goals give direction. Practice builds momentum.

The Hour of Power

In my own life, practice shows up in a ritual I call the "Hour of Power".

Each morning, I start the day with a 60-minute routine that supports my health and creativity:

- 10 minutes of meditation
- 20 minutes of yoga
- 30 minutes of strength or cardio training

Within three weeks, it became second nature. The result? I stay fit and focused without needing to obsess over metrics.

This principle applies equally to creative work. By establishing daily, weekly, or monthly rituals, we move from apprentice to expert in our chosen craft.

The Four Stages of Mastery

Whether you're a surgeon, sculptor, or salesperson, skill development follows four predictable stages:

1. **Unconscious Incompetence** – You don't know what you don't know. There's a kind of boldness here. Someone watches a world-class speaker or business leader and thinks, "I could do that." Then they try – and quickly realise there's more to it than meets the eye.

2. **Conscious Incompetence** – This is the humbling stage. You become painfully aware of how far you have to go. This is where most people quit.
   I remember watching top keynote speakers early in my career and feeling discouraged. How could I ever match their presence and precision? But I reminded myself not to compare my backstage to their onstage. As Michael Caine once said:
   "The rehearsal is the work. The performance is the play."

3. **Conscious Competence** – You can now do good work, but you have to think hard while doing it. A few years ago, I was in Recife, Brazil, to deliver a keynote to members of the Family Business Network (FBN). The night before, I got food poisoning. I could barely get out of bed. Ten minutes before showtime, I pulled myself together and gave the keynote. I barely remember it. But the audience was happy – and several attendees booked me for future events. I got through it because the foundation had been laid.

4. **Unconscious Competence** – This is mastery. When even at 70%, you're still capable of delivering 100% results. As a professional, your worst performance has to be better than an amateur's best performance. And here's the thing: people often accelerate through these stages faster when they practise alongside others – especially those operating at a higher level.

That's what practice builds: capability, under pressure.

Practice Shapes Identity

A practice isn't just something you do; it's something you become.

As author Austin Kleon says, "Lots of people want to be the noun without doing the verb. They want the job title without the work."

Too many people want to be writers without writing, they want to be speakers without speaking, they want to be creators without creating.

When I began writing 1,000 words a day, I stopped thinking of myself as someone who writes. I became a writer. The action reshaped the identity. And when others see you show up consistently, they start to trust and invest in your growth – making your practice a shared, social asset.

Creative Practice in a Modern World

The highest performers in any domain – design, law, tech, sales – don't rely on inspiration. They rely on systems.

- Writers measure word counts.
- Marketers track how many campaigns or creative tests they run.
- Sales leaders log how many questions they ask, pitches they rehearse, or prospects they reach out to.
- Engineers track problems solved, lines of clean code written, or peer reviews given.

And now, with AI tools, we can accelerate feedback loops even further. AI can analyse a presentation transcript in seconds, highlight unclear points, suggest alternatives, and even simulate audience reactions. We'll explore this Human+AI dimension of practice in a later chapter – but for now, understand this: AI doesn't replace practice. It makes good practice faster and bad practice impossible to hide.

Final Takeaway

Mastery doesn't come from talent. It comes from showing up. Not once. Not when you feel like it. But over and over again – until the motions you once had to think about become second nature.

Whether you're writing a book, delivering a keynote, launching a startup, or leading a team, your success won't be determined by goals alone. It will be shaped by the systems you build and the habits you honour. Goals set the destination. Practice is the vehicle that gets you there.

So don't just set the target. Build the system. Don't wait for motivation. Build the habit. Don't focus on performance. Focus on the practice.

And here's the secret: practice doesn't live in isolation. The most powerful habits are rarely solo acts. They are shaped by the people you work with, the feedback you receive, and the environment you create around yourself. A comedian needs an audience. A CEO needs a trusted inner circle. An athlete needs a coach. Even the most solitary creative work flourishes when it's supported by others.

That's why in the next chapter, we'll look at how to build relationships that sharpen your skills, challenge your assumptions, and multiply your results. Because when practice becomes shared – across people, processes, and places – that's when creativity stops being an individual pursuit and starts becoming a collective force.

Next Actions

Do This Week

1. **Design a Deliberate Practice Routine**
   Choose one skill you want to improve (e.g., presenting, coding, selling). Define a specific drill you can repeat daily or weekly that pushes you just beyond your current skill level. Build in immediate feedback – whether from a colleague, a mentor, or a tool.

2. **Run a Feedback Loop Sprint**
   Pick a current project and run it through three quick feedback cycles in a single week. Each time, implement changes before moving forward. Notice how much sharper your work becomes in less time.

Download the worksheet for this chapter on Practice as well as bonus content at www.supercreativitybook.com

Reflect and Reframe

Questions to Ask Yourself

- Where in my work am I relying on raw talent instead of structured practice?
- Which skills would benefit most from short, frequent feedback loops?
- If I had to design a "training plan" for my creativity, what would be my daily drills?
- How might AI tools help me simulate more practice reps or deliver faster feedback?

Key Takeaways

SuperCreator's Cheat Sheet
- Practice turns creativity from chance into choice.
- Deliberate practice means working at the edge of your abilities, with specific goals and fast feedback.
- Feedback loops shorten the path to mastery – especially when they're frequent and specific.
- Habits shape identity: you don't become a writer, speaker, or innovator by thinking about it. You do it by showing up.
- Human+AI feedback loops can accelerate skill growth, but only if the underlying practice is solid.
- Flow and mastery emerge when practice aligns with your purpose and personality.

PART 2

HUMAN+HUMAN CREATIVITY

"Alone we can do so little; together we can do so much." –
Helen Keller

Why Great Ideas Fail (and How to Fix It)

Here's something every leader already knows: ideas are worth
nothing without execution. A brilliant idea, poorly executed, is
just potential unrealised. But multiply a great idea with great
execution, and you have the power to revolutionise entire industries. And the engine that powers that execution? Better collaboration.

A few years ago, I was brought in to work with a leadership
team at a global healthcare company. The CEO had a bold vision
for a new patient care model – faster diagnosis, more personalised treatment, better outcomes. On paper, it sounded brilliant.
In practice, nothing was moving.

The problem wasn't the idea. The problem was the islands.
R&D worked in one silo, marketing in another, and operations
somewhere else entirely. Each group was brilliant on its own,
but without a bridge between them, progress stalled.

Then something changed. The company reorganised into small, cross-functional squads – each with a scientist, a marketer, a project manager, and a patient advocate. They shared data daily, solved problems in real time, and built trust. Within months, the first pilot program launched. Within a year, they were rolling out the model across the world.

Same people. Same resources. Same idea. The difference? Human+Human Creativity – the multiplier effect of people creating together.

The Three Forces Behind Creative Collaboration

In Part 1 of this book, we focused on building you – your **Purpose**, your **Personality**, and your **Practice**. That was the foundation. But personal mastery will only take you so far. At some point, the ceiling you hit won't be your own skill level – it'll be your ability to work with others.

That's where Human+Human comes in.

It's what happens when you combine your creativity with the creativity of others: colleagues, clients, communities, even competitors. It's the exponential lift that turns sparks into wildfires. It's the difference between ideas that live in your head and ideas that live in the world.

Collaboration takes many forms:

- A CEO and CFO aligning on a strategy that saves a company
- A product manager and a data scientist teaming up to design a new subscription model
- A mentor and mentee accelerating each other's growth
- A cross-functional team launching a new innovative product in record time

- Even a Human+Machine partnership where AI augments human judgment

But collaboration alone isn't enough. You can have a room full of geniuses and still get nowhere. To turn collaboration into innovation, you need three elements working in harmony:

People – the right mix of skills, perspectives, and energy.

Process – a clear system that moves ideas from spark to solution.

Place – an environment – physical, digital, and cultural – that makes creativity possible.

Miss one of these, and progress stalls. Get all three right, and you unlock an X-factor that accelerates everything.

Think of it as a creative operating system – not just for you, but for your team, your company, and even your industry. In the chapters ahead, we'll explore:

- **People** – how to find, develop, and collaborate with the right mix of minds.
- **Process** – how to design workflows that turn ideas into outcomes without killing creativity.
- **Place** – how to shape spaces, both physical and virtual, that spark better thinking.

Because creativity isn't just about having ideas, it's about executing them – at the right time, in the right way, with the right people.

This is Human+Human Creativity: the art and science of multiplying what's possible.

CHAPTER 4

PEOPLE (WHO ARE WE CREATING WITH)

"No one can whistle a symphony. It takes a whole orchestra to play it." – H.E. Luccock

James Watson and Francis Crick are widely credited with discovering the double-helix structure of DNA – a breakthrough that changed science forever. But that insight wouldn't have been possible without Rosalind Franklin, a brilliant X-ray crystallographer whose Photo 51 provided the critical evidence. Though she never collaborated with them directly and wasn't initially credited, her meticulous work was instrumental. Watson and Crick may have fit the mould of the classic scientific duo, but Franklin's contribution shows how many great discoveries depend on the unrecognised work of others.

That's the reality of creative work. It may start with one mind – but it rarely ends there.

In Part One of this book, we focused on the personal disciplines of creativity: how individuals generate, shape, and test ideas. But creativity doesn't thrive in isolation. It needs collaborators, critics, and supporters – the people who elevate, challenge, or refine our thinking. Whether you're designing a product, writing a report, or launching a business, who you create with matters just as much as what you create.

In this chapter, we shift from solo sparks to shared momentum. We'll explore how great ideas scale not just through process – but through people. This is where Human+Human Creativity begins.

We'll look at:

- How creative duos and "hidden contributors" shape extraordinary work
- What makes teams effective – not just in talent, but in trust
- Why psychological safety is a competitive advantage
- How tools like the Barbell Model and Virtual Advisory Boards support high-performing individuals and teams

Because behind every great idea is a network of people – some visible, some backstage – whose collaboration turns creativity into innovation.

Let's meet them.

CREATIVE PAIRS THE POWER OF TWO

"Everything that irritates us about others can lead us to an understanding of ourselves". - Carl Jung

The Power of Creative Pairing

There are two fun things to do when you visit the city of Stockholm. The first is to go to the ABBA Museum, where you can dress up like Benny, Björn, Agnetha, and Anni-Frid and sing along to "Dancing Queen". But afterwards, walk into the historic centre and visit the Nobel Prize Museum.

That museum celebrates some of the greatest thinkers and innovators in history. One of the first exhibits you'll come across is for Linus Pauling – one of the few people to win two Nobel

Prizes. A pioneer in quantum chemistry and molecular biology, Pauling had a sharp, analytical mind. But what caught my eye was the French beret he kept on his desk. He used it as a daily reminder: even in the world of equations and data, creativity and curiosity were essential. It was a symbol of duality – of being both a scientist and an artist.

What many don't realise is that Pauling's second Nobel – awarded for peace activism – was shaped in no small part by his wife, Ava. She wasn't just a supporter; she was a collaborator, critic, and moral compass. Historians now argue that the prize should have been awarded jointly. Ava was what we might call a "backstage hero" – one of the hidden figures whose influence is felt even when their name is missing from the official record.

Why Great Ideas Often Come in Pairs

Some of the greatest creative breakthroughs in history didn't come from huge teams – but from creative duos. Jobs and Wozniak. Lennon and McCartney. Marie and Pierre Curie. These partnerships worked not because the individuals were the same but because they were different in exactly the right ways.

Creative pairs often sit at a point of productive tension – visionary and implementer, dreamer and realist, provocateur and editor. Steve Jobs once said that Apple wouldn't exist without Wozniak's engineering mind. Later, his intense and sometimes volatile collaboration with Jony Ive drove Apple's golden design era. The two men had very different working styles, but their mutual respect and creative friction sharpened each other's thinking. They didn't dilute the work. They distilled it.

And the benefits of creative pairing aren't just anecdotal – they're backed by data. A study of more than 166,000 scientific collaborations found that long-term creative duos – what researchers call "super ties" – led to papers receiving 17% more citations on average than those written with one-off collaborators. Similarly, an analysis of nearly 20 million academic papers and over two million patents showed that team-authored work is cited more than twice as often as solo work. "Home run" breakthroughs – those cited over 100 times – were six times more likely to emerge from teams than individuals.

In business, the pattern holds. Research shows that 36% of a company's overall performance can be attributed to the strength of its internal collaborations. Pairing up effectively doesn't just spark better ideas – it drives better results.

Creative Tension Builds Better Thinking

In my own work, I've been fortunate to collaborate with people who elevate my thinking. During the writing of this book, there were moments when a simple comment or question from a creative partner forced me to rethink an entire section – or to strip away everything but the essence.

The most valuable collaborators aren't the ones who always agree with you. They're the ones who respect you enough to challenge your assumptions. It takes trust. It takes patience. And it takes a willingness to let go of ego in service of a better result.

When that dynamic is right, something extraordinary happens. The ideas get smarter. The work gets sharper. And the outcome becomes something neither person could have achieved alone.

The Barbell Model: Mentoring for Momentum

One of the most effective ways to build creative resilience is to surround yourself with the right creative pairings – especially across generations. I call it the Barbell Model of Mentorship.

On one end of the barbell is someone ahead of you – a mentor. They've already walked the road you're on. They can't give you all the answers, but they can help you avoid blind spots and navigate inflection points with more confidence. Their wisdom is a stabilising force.

On the other end is someone younger – or newer to your field. A mentee, yes, but also a creative partner with fresh eyes and fewer assumptions. They ask questions you've stopped asking. They help you stay curious. And what starts as a mentoring relationship often becomes mutual: you share experience, and they bring clarity and energy in return.

The result is balance. One end grounds you. The other lifts you. In between, you get stronger.

Find Your Creative Counterweight

So ask yourself: Who challenges you in the best possible way? Who do you trust enough to share early-stage ideas with – knowing they'll improve them, not just approve them?

And just as importantly, who might be behind your own success story – offstage, unseen, but essential?

Because sometimes, the key to unlocking your next breakthrough isn't doing more alone. It's doing better with someone else.

MOVING FROM "ME" TO "WE"

"Getting the right people and the right chemistry is more important than getting the right idea." – Ed Catmull

From Expertise to Orchestration

If creative pairs offer speed and trust, creative teams offer scale and complexity. But collaboration isn't additive. It's multiplicative. Innovation only happens when the space between people becomes catalytic. When their combined contributions create something that no one could have produced alone.

Consider the story of Professor John Wickham, a pioneer in keyhole surgery. Wickham began as a traditional surgical expert, perfecting his individual skills in the operating theatre. But his real breakthrough came when he shifted from personal mastery to systemic innovation.

Wickham realised that the future of surgery wouldn't be defined by how steady a surgeon's hands were, but by how well teams could collaborate. He built a cross-functional unit including a radiologist, a scrub nurse, an engineer, and a surgical instrument designer. This team, working in concert, radically reimagined surgical procedures. Smaller incisions, faster recovery, reduced risk. Not because of a single brilliant mind, but because multiple perspectives converged on a single problem.

This story was shared with me by Professor Roger Kneebone, author of Expert: Understanding the Path to Mastery, during his appearance on the SuperCreativity podcast. Kneebone uses Wickham's journey to highlight how true mastery often involves shifting from doing the work yourself to enabling and empowering others to excel.

Yet many in the surgical field resisted. They saw keyhole surgery as lesser because it didn't showcase the surgeon's virtuosity. But Wickham understood something deeper: mastery wasn't about individual heroism. It was about enabling better outcomes through collective intelligence.

Creative leadership isn't a solo act – it's a team function. Bain & Company's analysis of 1,250 companies found that businesses with strong, cohesive leadership teams consistently outperform their competitors in revenue growth, profitability, and shareholder return. Moreover, the style of leadership matters. Studies show that inclusive leadership – where leaders create openness and psychological safety – directly boosts employee innovation and leads to stronger organisational innovation performance.

Designing for Innovation

The shift from "me" to "we" as Professor Kneebone calls it isn't limited to medicine. In any creative domain, true innovation emerges when leaders stop trying to be the smartest in the room and start focusing on making the room smarter.

We see this mindset at work inside GCHQ, the UK's intelligence and cyber agency. There, innovation isn't accidental. It's architected. Mathematicians, linguists, hackers, behavioural scientists, and engineers are brought together to tackle complex problems as dynamic teams. People rotate roles. Silos are dissolved. Even sabbaticals are encouraged to keep thinking fresh.

I spoke with Robert Hannigan, former Director of GCHQ, on my SuperCreativity podcast. We discussed the idea in his book Counter-Intelligence, where he emphasised something that we learned earlier: the greatest breakthroughs don't come from lone geniuses. That's a Hollywood myth. Real innovation comes from structured collaboration. And GCHQ reflects this. Today, one in four of its team members is neurodivergent. Diversity isn't a quota, it's a strategy.

The same was true during World War II at Bletchley Park. Movies like The Imitation Game spotlight Alan Turing, and rightly so. But behind the legend were over 10,000 people, 76% of them women, working in parallel to break codes, run simulations, and imagine new ways to think. Genius didn't live in one mind. It lived in the network.

The Hidden Architecture of Collaboration

Teams that innovate aren't just thrown together. They're designed. Like a jazz ensemble, their brilliance lies in improvisation within shared structure. Everyone plays their part. But it's the interplay – the tension, the trust, the creative risk – that creates magic.

In today's world, that means moving beyond fixed hierarchies to fluid systems. Systems where leadership is contextual. Where designers lead on design. Where engineers drive technical constraints. Where insights don't always come from the top.

This is what it means to move from Me to We. To stop seeing creativity as a solo act and start seeing it as a collective performance. And while assembling the right people is critical, it's only the beginning. Because collaboration thrives – or dies – based on one invisible force: psychological safety.

That's where we go next.

INCLUSIVE INNOVATION AND PSYCHOLOGICAL SAFETY

"When people feel psychologically safe, they're more willing to take risks, admit mistakes, and share ideas – even when those ideas are half-formed or unconventional." – Amy Edmondson

Safety First: The Hidden Engine of Creative Teams

In the previous section, we explored the power of moving from solo brilliance to collaborative breakthroughs. But simply bringing people together isn't enough. To unlock collective intelligence, leaders must create an environment where individuals feel safe to contribute fully. This is where psychological safety comes in.

Psychological safety is the invisible infrastructure of high-performing teams. It's the shared belief that you won't be punished or humiliated for speaking up with ideas, questions, concerns, or mistakes. When people feel safe, they contribute. When they don't, they stay silent – and silence is the enemy of innovation.

It's easy to say, "Every idea matters", but unless people actually believe it, good ideas stay hidden. Creativity doesn't flourish in fear. It thrives in trust.

Kickbox: When Trust Comes in a Red Box

A compelling example of psychological safety in action comes from US software company Adobe. Faced with the challenge of accelerating innovation, Adobe realised it couldn't rely solely on top-down initiatives. So they launched a bold internal experiment called Kickbox – a program designed to democratise idea generation and give every employee a shot at innovation.

The kit itself looks simple: a red cardboard box labelled "Pull in case of idea." Inside was a thoughtfully curated toolkit for creative action: a manual, a notebook for "bad ideas", Post-it notes, a pen, a timer, a chocolate bar, a Starbucks gift card, and – most remarkably – a $1,000 prepaid debit card. No approvals. No expense reports. No permission required.

The message was clear: if you or your team have a problem to solve or an idea to develop then we are giving you permission.

Adobe distributed a thousand of these boxes globally. For the cost of a typical R&D project, the company seeded a thousand experiments. "We only need one to work for the program to pay for itself," said Adobe's leadership.

But the real genius wasn't in the box – it was in the trust it symbolised. By placing creative tools and financial autonomy directly in the hands of employees, Adobe wasn't just soliciting ideas. It was signalling belief. The company was saying: "We trust you. We think you're capable. And we're backing you."

Some of the most promising ideas were later invited to a second phase – symbolised by the mysterious Blue Box. Adobe hasn't revealed exactly what's inside (likely additional resources to make the idea a reality), but what it represents is clear: higher trust, greater support, and a defined path toward full development.

Scaling Innovation Starts with Trust

The Kickbox model has since been adopted by many of my clients including Cisco, Roche, and Caterpillar. Why? Because it proves a simple but radical truth: you don't need to wait for a top-down breakthrough. You can build a culture of innovation from the ground up – if you first build trust.

Google's landmark Project Aristotle study echoed this insight. After analysing hundreds of its internal teams, researchers found that psychological safety – not raw intelligence or experience – was the number one predictor of high team performance. When people feel safe, they create. When they're trusted, they try. And when organisations open the floor instead of guarding the mic, innovation shows up in places they never expected.

Inclusive innovation doesn't just mean inviting everyone to the table. It means giving them a budget, a toolkit, and the freedom to act. It's how you turn spectators into creators. And it's how you signal to your team – not with words, but with structure – that every voice matters.

So here's the question:

What would happen if you created the conditions where your quietest team members felt safe enough to speak their boldest ideas?

Because sometimes the most transformative voices aren't the loudest.

Sometimes, they're the ones still waiting to be heard.

Let's explore those people next – the backstage heroes and hidden figures whose impact shapes the outcomes, even if they rarely claim the spotlight.

BACKSTAGE HEROES

"The best ideas often come from the quietest voices."
– Susan Cain, author of *Quiet*

Every Organisation Has Its Unsung Heroes

Back when I was managing rock stars, I learned a truth that applies just as much to the corporate world as it does to the concert stage: the people who make the magic happen aren't always in the spotlight.

Sure, the lead singer gets the applause. But it's the lighting designer who creates the mood. The performance coach who sharpens the delivery. The tour manager who ensures the right gear shows up in the right city at the right time. These are the backstage heroes – the ones whose impact is undeniable, even if their names aren't up in lights.

The same dynamic exists in organisations. We celebrate founders and frontline innovators. But behind every product launch, every breakthrough, every customer experience, there are unsung contributors in cybersecurity, logistics, finance, and operations – quietly keeping things running, solving problems before they surface, and sometimes generating ideas that never get heard.

If we want to build truly innovative, resilient organisations, we can't just rely on the loudest voices or the most visible roles. We need to intentionally identify, support, and elevate those behind-the-scenes contributors whose work too often goes unnoticed. And that requires more than good intentions – it requires systems and structures that are designed to surface hidden potential. It requires a more inclusive style of innovation.

According to Accenture, nearly 50% of breakthrough innovations originate from employees outside formal R&D departments – often from individuals in overlooked or operational roles. That's half of your organisation's creative potential, waiting backstage.

Meet the Idea Matchmaker

Hewlett Packard Enterprise (HPE) took the idea of inclusive innovation and Human+Human collaboration even further with its Idea Matchmaker tool. Recognising that some of the most valuable innovations come not from traditional R&D departments but from individuals working "backstage" across their global organisation, they created a platform to surface and connect hidden talent.

Idea Matchmaker works like a modern dating app except for ideas. Rather than pairing employees based on job titles, departments, or geographic proximity, the AI system identifies individuals whose working styles, problem-solving approaches, and passions complement one another. It is, in essence, a matchmaking engine for creativity. It's an example of Human+Machine creative collaboration that you'll learn more about later.

The premise was simple but powerful: what if untapped creativity already existed within the organisation – waiting only to be discovered and activated?

Matching Minds, Not Just Roles

The system scans employee profiles, previous project contributions, collaboration patterns, and even internal messaging data (with permission) to suggest unexpected partnerships. The goal isn't to improve efficiency in existing roles. It's to create collisions. Intersections. New teams around new problems.

One pairing brought together an in-house lawyer in the U.S. and a tech lead in India. These two employees likely would never have met through traditional workflows. Yet, once connected by the platform, they created an internal tool to streamline cross-departmental communication. It was a small solution to a big problem – one that had long been ignored. The AI didn't just suggest a conversation. It seeded a collaboration that solved something real.

It's Not Just About Ideas. It's About Combinations.

This was the core insight behind the platform: creativity isn't just about brilliant ideas; it's about brilliant combinations. The Idea Matchmaker became a kind of social R&D layer inside HPE – a way to intentionally create diverse cognitive teams, often across time zones and functions, to tackle strategic or even unspoken problems.

The platform didn't just produce results. It changed how people felt about their ability to contribute. Employees who had once been excluded from strategic projects were now part of innovation teams. The quiet thinkers, the lateral minds, the people who never spoke up in town halls – they were being sought out and matched based on how they think, not how loudly they talk.

And while it was driven by artificial intelligence, the real power came from what it amplified: human connection. The AI wasn't there to replace creativity – it was there to enhance it. To notice the overlooked, to surface the invisible, to suggest what a human manager might never think to pair.

From Hierarchies to Human Networks

In doing so, it changed not just the flow of ideas, but the very structure of opportunity within the company.

We'll dive deeper into this interplay between human creativity and machine augmentation in the next section of the book on Human+Machine creative collaboration. But HPE's Idea Matchmaker gives us an early glimpse: when we stop relying solely on hierarchy and start designing networks of trust, curiosity, and complementarity, we don't just unlock new ideas. We find those backstage heroes in our organisation.

So here's a question worth asking yourself – and your team: Who in your organisation is doing brilliant work out of view? Who hasn't been asked for their ideas lately, but should be? And just as importantly, do we have the systems and processes in place to find, support, and reward these hidden figures and backstage heroes? Sometimes, the next big innovation doesn't come from the centre of the stage – but from the wings.

And while platforms like HPE's Idea Matchmaker help reveal hidden collaborators, we also need trusted circles to sharpen, support, and challenge our ideas over time. That's where the concept of a Braintrust comes in – a powerful structure you can build to surround yourself with constructive critics, advisors, and creative allies. Let's explore how to create your own.

BUILDING YOUR BRAINTRUST

Build a Board You Can Call on Anytime

Who do you call when your best idea starts to wobble?

Even solo projects need infrastructure – and that means feedback, challenge, and perspective. Especially when you're operating at the edge of your creativity.

When I began writing this book, I assembled what I call a virtual advisory board. Some were real – mentors like Elaine Pofeldt, a journalist who gave me ideas on how to structure the book, and David Avrin, a fellow speaker and author who pushed me on how to build a daily writing practice.

Others were virtual. I used generative AI to simulate the editorial voices of thinkers I respect – Ryan Holiday, Seth Godin, Jay Papasan. What would they say about this chapter structure? How would they critique this positioning? The results weren't perfect, but they were useful. The act of asking "What would X say?" opened me up to feedback I wasn't ready to hear yet from others. It helped me edit my own work before showing it to anyone else.

Want to build your own? I'll show you how to do this using AI in Part 4: Tools.

Who Gets a Seat at Your Table?

One exercise I often use with leadership teams is deceptively simple: list the five people you most often go to for input. Then ask:

- Do they challenge you enough?
- Do they think differently from you?
- Do they help you see what you're missing?

If the answer is "not really", you need to widen the circle.

Research from Google's Project Aristotle, which studied hundreds of high-performing teams, found that the highest functioning groups shared one essential characteristic: psychological safety. But beyond trust, the most innovative teams also embraced what's called creative abrasion – the ability to engage in vigorous debate, challenge assumptions, and explore opposing viewpoints without personal conflict.

Pixar institutionalised this idea through the Braintrust – a group of trusted creatives who provide blunt, candid, non-binding feedback to directors. The notes can be tough, but they're never personal. The director doesn't have to take the advice, but they're expected to seriously consider it. The Braintrust exists not to create consensus, but to eliminate blind spots.

This kind of systemised friction is what separates amateur creative teams from enduringly excellent ones. The right feedback at the right moment can save a bad idea – or transform a good one into something extraordinary.

Creative abrasion, when properly harnessed, helps teams move past politeness into productive challenge. In one study, teams that practiced high levels of creative abrasion outperformed others in both idea quality and execution, despite having more conflict. The key wasn't avoiding disagreement – it was learning to use it.

You don't need a Hollywood studio to do this. Your Braintrust might be made up of colleagues, clients, mentors – or even simulated voices that help sharpen your thinking.

From Solo Spark to Collective Intelligence

As this chapter has hopefully shown, creativity may start with an individual. But it doesn't stay there.

To go from spark to scale, you need partners. Collaborators. Contrarians. Amplifiers. You need structure and spontaneity. Friction and trust. You need systems that don't just permit creativity – but expect it.

That's the promise of Human+Human Creativity. Not just working together, but thinking together. Not just more voices, but better combinations.

So who's in your Braintrust?

In the next chapter, we'll return to the essential ingredient that transforms ideas into reality: Process. Because once the right people are in the room, the question becomes, How do you move from imagination to execution? That's where process comes in – not to stifle creativity, but to give it structure, momentum, and a path forward.

Next Actions

Do This Week

1. **Map Your Braintrust**
   List the five people you currently turn to for input or feedback. Now ask: who is missing? Add one person who challenges your assumptions and one who brings a fresh or unfamiliar perspective. Reach out to at least one of them this week.

2. **Run a Creative Friction Audit**
   Choose one current project and reflect: is there enough constructive tension in your team or collaborators? Are ideas being challenged productively – or is everyone playing it safe? Share this chapter with your team and invite one open conversation around feedback and creative abrasion.

3. **Create Your Virtual Advisory Board**
   Pick three thinkers you admire (living or dead). In your notebook or a doc, write their names and ask: "What would they say about this idea, structure, or pitch?" Use this exercise to refine a project you're working on this week.

Download the worksheet for this chapter on People as well as bonus content at www.supercreativitybook.com

Reflect and Reframe

Questions to Ask Yourself

- Who regularly makes my thinking sharper? Who have I outgrown – or who no longer stretches me?
- Am I surrounding myself with people who bring friction *and* trust – or just agreement?
- What hidden figures in my life or work have contributed significantly without credit?
- Do my teams and collaborations reflect real cognitive diversity – or just cosmetic difference?
- How am I actively designing moments for unexpected perspectives to enter the room?

Key Takeaways

SuperCreator's Cheat Sheet

- Creativity scales through people – not just more people, but *better combinations*.
- Creative pairs thrive on tension, trust, and complementary skills. They sharpen each other, not smooth each other out.
- Great teams are designed, not defaulted. The right mix of disciplines and perspectives multiplies innovation.
- Creative abrasion – the respectful clash of ideas – leads to better outcomes. Comfort rarely produces breakthroughs.

- Psychological safety is essential. Without it, even brilliant minds will hold back.
- Hidden contributors often carry breakthrough insights. Shine a light backstage.
- Braintrusts, mastermind groups, and structured feedback loops are essential tools for sustainable creative growth.
- The shift from solo genius to collaborative catalyst is the bridge to mastery.

CHAPTER 5

PROCESS (HOW WE CREATE)

"Process isn't the enemy of creativity – it's what gives your ideas a chance to survive." – Ed Catmull

Look around you for a moment. What do you see? Maybe you're in a coffee shop, or on a plane, or out walking. Now focus on something man-made: a coffee mug, a cake, a watch, a book, your phone, the chair you're sitting on.

That object didn't appear by magic. It exists because a group of people collaborated to make it real. Designers sketched it. Engineers built it. Marketers positioned it. Someone sold it. Someone else delivered it. What you're holding, reading, eating or resting on is the result of a sophisticated process – one that may have involved tens, hundreds, or even thousands of people working across time zones, disciplines, and stages of development.

Creativity is bringing new things to mind. Innovation is bringing new things into the world. And what transforms a creative idea into an innovative product or service is process.

That's what this chapter is about.

The creative process is the sequence of steps we follow to generate, develop, and ultimately execute on an idea. Over the years, hundreds of books have tried to explain creativity. But strip away the jargon, and you'll find one time-tested framework – a five-stage process that helps us turn problems into solutions:

1. **Preparation**
2. **Incubation**
3. **Insight**
4. **Evaluation**
5. **Elaboration**

Mastering each stage won't just make you more creative – it will make your ideas more actionable. While the process is often presented as linear, in practice it's more circular. A breakthrough in elaboration might send you back to preparation. Each phase feeds the next. Each stage poses different questions to be answered.

Let's begin – where all creative work begins – with Preparation.

THE PREPARATION STAGE

Clients bring me in to deliver keynotes, facilitate workshops, or advise their leadership teams not just because they have problems to solve but because they have opportunities to seize. Sometimes they're facing complexity, uncertainty, or disruption and need help finding a way through. Other times, they've spotted a moment of potential – an emerging market, a creative idea within their team, or a new technology – and they want to unlock it before their competitors do.

That's the nature of modern creativity. It's not only about fixing what's broken – it's about finding what's possible. There's a fundamental difference between problem-solving and problem-finding. Problem-solving is linear: identify the issue, apply a solution. But problem-finding is exploratory. It's where real breakthroughs happen – when we learn to see challenges, questions, or possibilities others have missed.

And whether we're solving or finding, the process begins in the same place: Preparation.

Immerse First, Create Later

Preparation is about immersion. It's the stage where you dig into your field, absorb its nuances, and begin to understand the landscape before trying to reshape it. In business, this could mean analysing customer behaviour, studying competitor strategies, or reviewing past campaigns. A strategist might dive into market data. A product manager interviews users. An engineer pulls apart a failed prototype to uncover hidden insights.

At this stage, you're not trying to come up with solutions – you're trying to ask better questions. Why did this project work in one market but fail in another? What patterns are emerging that no one else is seeing? What assumptions are we clinging to that might be outdated?

Whether your drive is to fix something broken or explore something new, this phase is about developing what designers call informed intuition. The more you absorb, the sharper your instincts become.

And where you do this work matters. Preparation benefits from focused solitude. It's the executive blocking out an hour to reflect with a whiteboard. The marketing lead pouring over brand audits in a quiet office. The entrepreneur doing deep competitive research in a tucked-away corner of a coffee shop. When you carve out space for deep work, you start to tune your attention more effectively.

Gather Dots Before You Connect Them

Preparation also means documenting what you discover – before it disappears. I've learned to always carry tools for capturing thoughts in the moment. For me, it's a hybrid system: a notebook for real-time insights, Evernote for research articles, mind maps and Generative AI tools for structuring ideas, and voice notes when I'm on the move. What matters most isn't the tool, but the habit.

Professionals who create consistently aren't waiting for inspiration to strike. They're actively preparing for it. They're collecting raw material – dots – that will later be connected in surprising ways. Without this commitment to preparation, creativity becomes sporadic. With it, it becomes repeatable.

The biggest mistake most people make is rushing this stage – assuming they already know what they need to know and jumping straight to ideation or execution. But thoughtful preparation isn't wasted time. It's the foundation that supports every insight, breakthrough, and solution to come.

So take your time. Immerse yourself. Ask sharper questions. Zoom out before you zoom in. Because every meaningful idea starts with the decision to prepare well.

THE INCUBATION STAGE

> *"The most creative people have learned to tolerate the discomfort of not solving a problem right away. Their solutions are more original because they put in more pondering time."* – John Cleese

In our always-on culture, pausing can feel like weakness. We're taught to move fast, fill every minute, and push through ambiguity. But creativity doesn't always reward speed. It rewards timing – and timing depends on knowing when to act and when to step back.

That's what makes the incubation stage so counterintuitive – and so powerful.

Incubation is what happens when we stop consciously working on a problem. It's the phase where our minds shift from analysis to synthesis – where the raw material gathered during preparation begins to connect in surprising, subconscious ways. It might look like stillness, but beneath the surface, something important is happening.

In business, incubation often gets mistaken for inaction. A team launches a brainstorming session, generates a list of ideas, and wants to move straight to execution. But the best insights usually come not from pressing harder but from stepping back. This is the phase where deep creative breakthroughs begin to take shape, quietly and invisibly.

Defocusing: What John Cleese Taught Me About Creativity

I once had the opportunity to meet John Cleese of Monty Python fame at The Grand Hotel in Stockholm, and our conversation inevitably turned to a keynote he had given a few years earlier on the creative process. What struck me most was not the humour in his talk (though that was there in abundance), but his deeply reflective approach to creativity. He described what he called defocusing – the deliberate act of stepping away from a problem in order to allow the unconscious mind to work on it. "The moment you stop trying so hard," he said, "is often the moment the solution presents itself."

Cleese wasn't alone in this observation. From Einstein to Maya Angelou, many highly productive creators have remarked on the value of walking away. Creativity, it seems, requires intervals of looseness – periods where linear thought is suspended and associations are allowed to drift.

My father, a jazz guitarist, used to daydream as a schoolboy in England. His teachers mistook it for distraction, but his mind was already in Paris, picturing himself performing in smoky Left Bank clubs. He could see the stage, feel the strings beneath his fingers, hear the applause. In hindsight, that was a form of creative rehearsal – visioning without forcing. A mental sketch of a life not yet lived.

That's what incubation looks like: drifting, but with direction.

These kinds of mental meanderings are far from useless. Psychologist Jonathan Schooler has shown that mind-wandering is positively correlated with creative output – when our brain has time and space to roam, it often yields solutions that structured thinking alone can't produce.

In corporate settings, this matters just as much. I once worked with a startup founder who was overthinking her customer onboarding process. After weeks of whiteboarding, she went for a walk in a nearby park – no email, no doom-scrolling, just trees and time. Somewhere along that trail, the solution arrived. Not because she pushed harder, but because she gave her mind the freedom to breathe.

Mind-wandering, nature, and strategic rest aren't distractions from creative work. They are creative work.

But here's the challenge: most of us live on what Paul Graham calls Manager's Time: 15- or 30-minute calendar blocks optimised for meetings, tasks, and outputs. Incubation doesn't fit into that structure. It requires what Graham calls Maker's Time: long, uninterrupted stretches where nothing seems to be happening but everything important is actually being processed.

For creative work to flourish, you have to guard your Maker's Time ruthlessly. This is when deep ideas surface, patterns emerge, and clarity arrives – often not in front of a screen, but while walking, cycling, or doing something completely unrelated to the problem at hand.

How to Design for Incubation

Incubation doesn't just happen. Like any stage of the creative process, it can be supported, protected, and even designed. Here are four strategies that make space for it:

- **Pre-load a question before sleep.** At West Point Military Academy, cadets are taught to reflect on a challenge, write it down, then let it go. Neuroscience confirms this: the brain keeps working while we sleep. Solutions often appear in the morning with surprising clarity.
- **Practice defocused downtime.** Walk without headphones. Cook without a podcast. Commute in silence. These seemingly unproductive moments are often when the mind assembles ideas in the background.
- **Try Morning Pages.** Popularised by Julia Cameron, this practice involves writing three unfiltered pages first thing in the morning. It clears mental clutter and lets unexpected ideas rise to the surface. I often find that something useful – sometimes brilliant – emerges by page two.
- **Track your patterns.** When do your best ideas come? For some it's long walks, for others it's late nights, or

solo travel. Identify what works for you and build intentional incubation into your rhythm.

One caveat: during incubation, limit new inputs. Reading another book, loading up on research, or opening five browser tabs may feel productive, but it clutters the creative field. Incubation works best with stillness and simplicity.

Above all, be patient. Incubation doesn't have a progress bar. You don't see the connections being made. But when the solution arrives – often in the shower, on a walk, or as you wake – it feels complete, as if it was waiting for you to notice it.

That moment of recognition is your cue: you've entered the next stage of the creative process – Insight.

THE INSIGHT STAGE

"The best ideas come when you allow the stupid
ones to show up first." – Tina Fey

Not long ago, I was facilitating an innovation workshop in Paris for the leadership team of a global logistics company. Their challenge: how to streamline onboarding for thousands of warehouse employees across multiple regions. Despite strategy sessions, whiteboarding, and even hiring a consultancy, the team couldn't land on a solution that felt both scalable and simple.

On the first day of the workshop, I had shared a concept that seemed to resonate with the group – the idea that creativity isn't always about pushing harder, but about stepping back. I introduced them to the concept of incubation: how our most powerful insights often emerge not in moments of intense focus, but during moments of rest or routine – when the mind is free to connect dots in the background.

The next morning, one of the operations managers decided to go for an early run along the Seine before the day's session began. No agenda. Just movement, rhythm, and a mind still digesting the previous day's discussions. Somewhere between Pont Neuf and the Musée d'Orsay, it hit her – not a brand-new idea, but a new arrangement of everything they already had. The tools and training materials existed; what was missing was the sequence and simplicity.

That afternoon, she sketched out a modular onboarding model that reordered their existing resources into a more elegant flow. Within weeks, it had become the company's new global standard.

That's insight.

It often arrives in silence. But it is almost never random. Insight is the reward for earlier stages of the process – the questions asked in Preparation, the material absorbed, and the space created through Incubation. What feels like a sudden breakthrough is often just the mind finally catching up to itself.

You Can't Force It, But You Can Invite It

Insight is often misunderstood as a spontaneous breakthrough. But in truth, it's less like lightning and more like light finally being switched on in a room you've already spent time arranging. The brain has been working in the background – connecting, re-organising, filtering – until a new configuration clicks into place.

Neuroscientists John Kounios and Mark Beeman have shown that insight tends to strike when the brain is in a relaxed, alpha-wave state – calm, slightly detached, and inwardly focused. This is why ideas often emerge when we're walking, showering, cooking, or commuting. Our attention has loosened. We've stopped over-controlling our thoughts. The subconscious is free to assemble connections.

In the morning, especially, the brain is unwound and open. Alpha waves ripple across the right hemisphere. The self-critical part of the brain – the voice that says "that's a stupid idea" – hasn't fully woken up. This is why techniques like pre-loading questions before sleep, or doing Morning Pages first thing, are so powerful. They create a soft mental focus – a gateway to insight.

Personally, I often find insights while cycling in the Scottish Highlands or walking alone on London's Hampstead Heath. They don't arrive as fragments – they arrive as full arcs. The shape of a keynote, the hook of a pitch, the structure of a chapter. Complete. Coherent. Waiting to be caught.

Protect the Fragility of Ideas

The problem with insight is its fragility. It can feel so vivid and permanent in the moment – and then vanish completely. That's why you need a system to catch it the second it shows up.

It doesn't have to be fancy. A notebook by your bed. A voice memo app on your phone. A Google Doc with no structure. The key is immediacy. Don't rely on memory. Insight is perishable.

One method I use is what I call an Insight Inbox – a simple note category where I drop any flashes or unexpected connections. No editing. No overthinking. Just a container to hold the idea until I'm ready to sort it.

Another tip: don't dismiss ideas that seem "too obvious". Many of the best insights feel simple in hindsight. That's a feature, not a flaw. It means your brain has done its work – processed the noise and clarified the signal. Simple doesn't mean shallow. It means integrated.

In fact, some of the most elegant breakthroughs in business, art, and science share this quality. They resolve tension not through complexity, but through clarity. That quiet "of course" feeling is often your cue that an idea is ready.

Stimulants and States of Mind

Even your brain chemistry plays a role. Neuroscience professor Martha Farah has studied the effects of stimulants like caffeine, Adderall, and Ritalin on cognitive performance. Her findings? These substances may help you stay focused and power through tasks – but they tend to suppress insight.

"You might be able to work eight hours straight," she says, "but you're probably not going to have many big insights."

Caffeine narrows focus. Insight needs looseness. That doesn't mean you have to give up your morning espresso – it just means you should be strategic. Use stimulants such as coffee when you need to execute. But when you want to ideate, leave room for wandering.

Sometimes, the best creative work happens when you're not trying so hard to create.

From Spark to Scrutiny

Not every insight deserves action. Some need testing. Others need time. Some will fade by morning, and that's okay. The point of this stage isn't to act on every idea. It's to recognise when something meaningful is trying to emerge.

When that shift from uncertainty to clarity happens – whether mid-sentence, mid-shower, or mid-stride – don't ignore it. Stop. Write. Reflect. Catch it before it escapes.

Because insight doesn't happen often. But when it does, it can change everything.

THE EVALUATION STAGE

"Focus is about saying no to the hundred other good ideas. You have to pick carefully. I'm as proud of the things we haven't done as the things I have done. Innovation is saying no to 1,000 things." – Steve Jobs

If incubation is about letting ideas rise, then evaluation is about deciding which ones deserve to land.

Most individuals and teams don't struggle with a lack of ideas – they struggle with what to do next. How do you move from possibility to priority? How do you choose which idea to bet on?

This is where creativity meets clarity. Where divergent thinking must give way to deliberate decision-making. But that transition only works if you've taken the time to explore properly first.

From Brainstorm to Breakthrough

One of the most common places where evaluation begins is in a brainstorming session. But far too often, brainstorming collapses under its own vagueness. A group is pulled into a room. There's no defined problem. The conversation gets hijacked by the most confident voice. Ideas are thrown out, but few are explored or evaluated properly.

The original idea behind brainstorming, coined by advertising executive Alex Osborn in the 1940s, was to generate lots of ideas by leveraging group diversity. But Osborn never intended for brainstorming to be chaotic. In fact, done well, brainstorming is structured exploration.

The key is to start not with answers but with questions.

As Peter Drucker once said: "The most common source of mistakes in management decisions is the emphasis on finding the right answer rather than the right question."

Before your team generates ideas, give them space to ask better ones. What exactly are we solving? What assumptions are we making? Who is this idea really for?

And remember: a brainstorming team is not the same as a committee. In brainstorming, the goal is exploration, not compromise. As Sir Barnett Cocks once said: "A committee is a cul-de-sac down which ideas are lured and then quietly strangled."

Protect your boldest ideas by giving them room to breathe before you judge them. Then, when the time comes to decide, shift gears with intention.

How to Evaluate Ideas with Clarity

Once the ideas are on the table, it's time to prioritise. Whether you're working solo or in a team, a structured framework can help you separate signal from noise.

One tool I often use is a simple scorecard. Rate each idea on a 1–10 scale across five criteria:

- **Novelty** – Is the idea original or unexpected?
- **Importance** – Does it address a meaningful problem?
- **Feasibility** – Can we execute with available resources?
- **Strategic Fit** – Does it align with our mission or goals?
- **Potential Impact** – Could it deliver measurable value?

This doesn't need to be overly scientific. You're not looking for mathematical certainty at this stage. You're looking for strategic clarity.

Say you're a fintech company weighing three directions: launching a podcast, building a customer referral engine, or expanding into a new market. Score each option and patterns will emerge. What looked equal on paper may reveal itself in the numbers.

Still can't decide? Try the "Hell Yes or No" filter, from entrepreneur Derek Sivers. If it doesn't energise you – or your team – it's a no.

Better Evaluation Starts with Better Framing

One of the most effective models I've seen comes from Amazon. Before any major decision-making meeting, the convener writes a detailed six-page narrative memo explaining the problem, the context, relevant data, and trade-offs. The first 30 minutes of the meeting are spent reading it – in silence. Only then does discussion begin.

The result? Fewer knee-jerk reactions. Better questions. More thoughtful evaluation.

This method works because it slows people down just enough to think clearly. It prioritises depth over volume, framing over theatrics. And it ensures everyone enters the conversation on equal informational footing.

Evaluating When You're Solo

But what if you're not working with a team? What if you're a solo creator or entrepreneur trying to assess your own ideas?

In these cases, I recommend building a Virtual Advisory Board – a technique I mentioned earlier. It combines trusted real-world mentors with imagined voices – people you admire, living or dead, real or fictional – who can help push your thinking.

You'll find a step-by-step guide for creating your own Virtual Advisory Board in Part 4: Tools.

From Possibility to Momentum

Evaluation is the moment when creativity gets serious. When we shift from possibility to priority. It's where we ask not What could we do? but What will we commit to doing?

This is the transition point between the idea and its implementation. Between having a dozen possibilities and choosing one path.

But the process doesn't stop with selection. Once the decision is made, you must move forward – and that means shaping the idea into something others can see, test, build, and believe in.

That's the job of the next stage in the creative process: Elaboration.

THE ELABORATION STAGE

> *"Genius is 1% inspiration and 99% perspiration."*
> – Thomas Edison

By this point in the creative process, you've laid the foundation. You've gathered insights (Preparation), allowed for reflection (Incubation), welcomed breakthrough moments (Insight), and filtered ideas through scrutiny (Evaluation). Now comes the moment of truth: building something real.

This is Elaboration – the stage where ideas are tested, shaped, and refined through execution. It's where imagination meets implementation.

People often over-glorify the aha! moment, but insight is usually the shortest part of the journey. Most of the work – most of the value – happens here, in the slow, iterative grind of making something actually function in the real world.

In movies, elaboration gets reduced to a montage. In life, it's measured in spreadsheets, prototypes, drafts, feedback loops, and quiet hours of effort. It's rarely glamorous. But it's essential.

Staying Open as You Build

Elaboration requires a paradoxical mindset: firm in direction, flexible in detail. You need conviction to keep going – but enough humility to adjust as you learn.

I once worked with a European fintech company developing an onboarding experience for new clients. They'd spent weeks mapping the customer journey on whiteboards. But when they launched the first version, confusion reigned. Clients dropped off halfway through the process. Instead of scrapping everything, they re-examined the friction points, adjusted the flow, rewrote the copy, and tested again. By the third iteration, conversion had tripled.

That's elaboration. It's not about being right the first time. It's about staying open long enough to get it right over time.

And here's a hard but liberating truth: feedback isn't failure. When something doesn't land the way you hoped, that's not a dead end – it's information. A data point. A message from your user, your audience, or the market.

Your job is to listen. Then adapt.

Why We Build MVPs

One of the most effective tools for navigating elaboration is the Minimum Viable Product (MVP) – popularised by Eric Ries in The Lean Startup and widely used in innovation hubs like Silicon Valley.

As Eric discussed when he was a guest on the SuperCreativity podcast, an MVP is not about cutting corners. It's about learning quickly. It's a rough version of your idea that includes just enough functionality to test your assumptions.

The process is simple:

1. **Identify the Problem and Audience** – What are you solving, and for whom?
2. **Define Core Features** – What's essential to deliver value?
3. **Build a Simple Prototype** – Create a rough, usable version.
4. **Launch and Test** – Get it in front of a small but relevant group.
5. **Measure Feedback** – Analyse usage, behaviour, and responses.
6. **Iterate** – Improve based on what you've learned. Repeat.

Take Buffer, the social media scheduling tool. Its founders started with just a landing page. It explained the product concept and included a "pricing" button. When visitors clicked it, they saw a message: "We're not ready yet – leave your email if you're interested." Only after they validated interest did they build the product.

This lean cycle – build, measure, learn – is the heartbeat of elaboration. It keeps you agile, responsive, and honest.

I Fall in Love Too Easily

As you start building, something wonderful happens: momentum. But that can also bring risk. When you become emotionally attached to your original version, you can lose objectivity.

This is where the creative principle "kill your darlings" becomes essential. The feature you love most might be what's holding the whole thing back. That section of the presentation you're obsessed with? It might be the thing confusing your audience.

Ask yourself regularly: Am I protecting this because it's right – or because it's mine?

Elaboration is about making the idea stronger. Not protecting your ego.

The Dip vs. the Dead End

At some point, the energy dips. Enthusiasm fades. Results stall. People don't "get" it. You hit resistance.

This is what Seth Godin calls The Dip – that tough stretch between the thrill of starting and the reward of finishing. It's uncomfortable. But it's also a sign of progress.

The challenge is knowing when you're in a dip – and when you've hit a dead end.
Ask:

- Am I still learning from the process?
- Is the core idea sound, even if the execution is wobbly?
- Are the obstacles external – or internal (like fear or fatigue)?
- Can I improve this with iteration – or is it fundamentally flawed?

A dip calls for resilience. A dead end calls for a rethink. Elaboration helps you tell the difference.

Rinse and Repeat

The creative process is not a straight line. It loops. It zigzags. Sometimes you discover an insight while building. Sometimes you evaluate mid-incubation. That's OK.

The five stages – Preparation, Incubation, Insight, Evaluation, Elaboration – aren't rigid steps. They're a flexible rhythm you'll return to over and over again.

But even the best ideas, shaped through process and refined through iteration, don't exist in a vacuum. Where we work – and the environments we create around us – can either accelerate or stifle that progress. Because creativity isn't just shaped by what we do or who we do it with, but where we do it. That's where we turn next.

Next Actions

Do This Week

1. Prepare with Purpose
    Choose one challenge or opportunity in your business. Instead of searching for answers, spend 45–60 minutes collecting questions. What's unclear? What are the underlying assumptions? Who's already trying to solve this? Use tools like search, customer interviews, or internal data. Then summarise your findings in a short "Curiosity Brief".

2. Schedule Your Incubation Time
    Block two 30–45-minute sessions this week for "defocused downtime". Go for a walk without headphones, take a silent commute, or try Morning Pages. Give your mind space to connect dots.

3. Start Your Insight Inbox
    Create a simple, frictionless way to capture flashes of insight. This could be a physical notebook, a voice memo

app, or a Google Doc titled "Spark File". Use it daily this week.

4. Evaluate with Clarity

   Use the five-question scorecard (Novelty, Importance, Feasibility, Strategic Fit, Potential Impact) to evaluate a list of ideas you've generated recently. Identify one "Hell, yes" project to move forward with.

5. Build and Test a Tiny MVP

   Turn that idea into something real. Don't overbuild. Create the leanest most basic version possible version (landing page, draft script, prototype) and share it three to five trusted people for feedback.

Download the worksheet for this chapter on Process as well as bonus content at www.supercreativitybook.com

Reflect and Reframe

Questions to Ask Yourself

- Am I spending enough time preparing or am I rushing toward execution?
- When do I naturally have my best ideas? How can I protect that time better?
- Do I consistently capture my insights, or am I losing valuable ideas because I assume I'll remember them later?
- Which idea am I clinging to because it's "mine", even if it's not working?
- Am I in a dip or a dead end? What's the honest signal telling me to do?

Key Takeaways

SuperCreator's Cheat Sheet

- **Creativity without process is potential without power.** The five stages – Preparation, Incubation, Insight, Evaluation, and Elaboration – form a reliable rhythm for turning ideas into impact.
- **Great preparation means absorbing deeply and asking sharper questions.** Creativity starts with immersion, not answers.
- **Incubation is not procrastination.** Your brain does its best work when you give it time, space, and stillness.
- **Insight often feels like remembering, not discovering.** It's the quiet click that comes from a well-prepared and well-rested mind.
- **Better brainstorming starts with better questions.** Don't just generate answers – curate the right prompts. Use frameworks like Curious Questions (see Part 4: Tools).
- **Evaluation is the hinge between dreaming and doing.** Use scorecards, memos, and your own Virtual Advisory Board to sort the signal from the noise.
- **Elaboration is the grind where ideas become reality.** Build, test, refine, repeat. Don't fall in love too early. Don't quit too soon.
- **Process is not the enemy of creativity.** It's what gives your best ideas a chance to survive – and thrive.

CHAPTER 6

PLACE (WHERE YOU CREATE)

"The space you work in can be just as important as the work itself." – Sir Norman Foster

Creativity doesn't happen in a vacuum. It's not just a function of individual talent or group dynamics. It's also shaped by where we create.

Walk into a jazz club in New Orleans, a research lab at MIT, or a design studio in Tokyo, and you'll feel it immediately. A sense of presence. Mood. Intention. Something more than just bricks, desks, and light fittings. The Romans had a phrase for this: Genius Loci – the spirit of a place.

In every truly creative space, you'll find one.

We often think of creativity as something in us. But the best creators also understand how to draw it from the world around them. They pay attention to environment – not just for aesthetics or productivity, but because they know that place collaborates with process. That where you work changes how you work.

In this chapter, we explore the silent influence of space and setting. From third places and creative sanctuaries to home set-ups and innovation hubs, we'll look at how intentional environments can unlock deeper focus, faster collaboration, and bolder thinking.

Because whether you're writing a book from a cabin in the Highlands, ideating in a coffee shop, or mapping your company's future in a boardroom, the room is always shaping the outcome.

Let's meet the genius in the room.

The Genius in the Room

*"Every place has a soul. Learn to listen, and
it will tell you how to create."*

What if your best collaborator isn't a person but a place?

Throughout history, some of the greatest ideas have emerged not just because of who was involved, but where they were. The Royal Society in seventeenth-century London. The Bauhaus studios in Weimar Germany. The garage where Hewlett and Packard built their first product. These places didn't just host creativity, they accelerated it.

That's the essence of Genius Loci – the belief that every environment holds a spirit or character that shapes the ideas formed within it.

It's a powerful idea, and a deeply practical one. When a space is designed with creativity in mind – whether it's a conference room, café, or mountaintop – it invites different kinds of thinking. It becomes a partner in the creative process.

Think of the spaces where you've had your best ideas. Maybe it was while walking in nature, working in a specific library, or sitting at your usual corner seat in a local café. These places carry more than just memories – they carry momentum. Something about them makes you more you.

This is why successful creators often build rituals around place. Maya Angelou rented hotel rooms to write. Mark Zuckerberg holds walking meetings. David Lynch visited the same diner every day to think. It's not just about habit – it's about activating a spatial relationship with their creativity.

You don't need a historic studio or famous desk to benefit from this. You just need to start paying attention to the creative energy of the places you already inhabit. The light, the sound, the objects. What helps you go deep? What pulls you out?

Because when you find a space that supports your thinking, something extraordinary happens.

It stops being just a location.

It becomes a collaborator.

THE THIRD PLACE: WHERE CREATIVITY MEETS COMMUNITY

"We shape our buildings; thereafter they shape us."
– Winston Churchill

The Power of Place in Shaping Creativity

Sociologist Ray Oldenburg coined the term third place to describe environments that are neither home (the first place) nor work (the second place), but where people gather informally to exchange ideas, build relationships, and foster community. These spaces are accessible, neutral, and filled with a steady mix of people. More importantly, they are fertile ground for creativity.

The concept is centuries old. In the fifteenth century, the first coffee houses – qahveh khaneh – appeared in Mecca and Medina. They quickly became hubs of storytelling, poetry, and debate. The idea spread across the Ottoman Empire and into Europe, where coffee houses evolved into something much more than places to drink coffee: they became incubators of culture, politics, and innovation.

Where Ideas Brewed: Cafes and Salons

In seventeenth-century Vienna, cafes became the beating heart of intellectual life. They weren't just cafés; they were what we might call "creativity clubs". Inside, kreis – discussion circles – gathered to debate philosophy, politics, art, and science. Over steaming cups of tea and sat around circular tables, ideas were tested, refined, and launched into the world.

When I visited Café Central and Café Landtmann in Vienna after giving a keynote on the future of manufacturing in Europe, I was struck by the atmosphere. To sit at those marble tables was to feel part of a centuries-long conversation. Trotsky, Stalin, Freud, Mahler, Dietrich, and countless poets and thinkers once argued and imagined in that same room. You could almost sense the collective consciousness of the place – the accumulated weight of thousands of minds sharpening ideas across generations. That is the genius loci – the spirit of place – that influences and inspires those who enter it.

These third places took many forms. In Paris, salons brought together artists and philosophers under gilded ceilings. In London, pubs doubled as political laboratories. In America, diners, jazz clubs, speakeasies and community halls became informal stages for creativity and social change. Each variation served as a cultural crossroads, where the value of your ideas outweighed your title or role.

Designing for Serendipity and Circles of Trust

From the very beginning, the architecture of these spaces mattered. Ancient Greek symposiums were literally structured around circles – gatherings where thinkers debated ideas that would become the foundations of Western civilisation. The word symposium itself comes from the Greek symposium, meaning "to drink together". The Greeks understood that sometimes a shared glass of wine could loosen boundaries, lubricate conversation, and make the creative process flow!

Long before symposiums, humans gathered around campfires. The circle equalised. No one sat at the head of the table. Everyone could see and be seen. This geometry created safety, intimacy, and exchange – the conditions under which creativity flourishes. As the Lakota spiritual leader Black Elk once said, "Everything the power of the world does is done in a circle."

But let me contrast the concept of a third space for creative collaboration with the Cabinet Room at No. 10 Downing Street in London. This is where British prime ministers have held meetings and made decisions for centuries. If you walk into the room you'll notice a couple of things. One big, long rectangular table and no live data being displayed anywhere in the room. In a room like this those who speak the loudest or most forcefully will win. Not necessarily those with the best ideas. Traditional rooms like this are for command and control not for creative collaboration. Lawyers love rooms like this.

Modern companies are rediscovering this principle. Steve Jobs designed Pixar's headquarters around a vast central atrium to force spontaneous encounters. Bloomberg's London headquarters features ramps and circular layouts intended to maximise collisions between teams. If you want to think outside the box, stop working inside one. Microsoft even built "treehouses" on its Redmond campus – elevated meeting spaces in the forest canopy – to offer employees a third place that blends nature, informality, and creativity.

And the data supports this. A University of Cambridge study found that teams exposed to informal social mixing in "third places" were 20% more likely to generate breakthrough ideas than those confined to traditional office settings. Creativity, it seems, thrives in spaces designed for serendipity.

The Third Place Reimagined for a New Era

Today, third places are being reimagined. Post-pandemic, companies are redesigning offices to function less as rows of desks and more as hubs of collaboration. Coworking spaces like We-Work or The Wing are built entirely on third-place principles: neutrality, flexibility, and community. Cafés remain fertile ground for individual focus amid communal hum.

And yet – even with these advances – there remains something irreplaceable about gathering in person. Screens can connect, but they rarely replicate the full energy of human presence, the subtle cues of body language, or the serendipity of an overheard conversation that sparks an idea. A handshake, a laugh, or even the silence of thinking together around a table creates a resonance that no virtual space can quite emulate.

The virtual world has offered alternatives. Recently, I delivered a keynote for Electronic Arts, the makers of FIFA and Call of Duty. For many who grew up gaming online – or for Gen Z students whose education was shaped by Zoom and Teams – the "third place" has migrated to digital spaces. Films like Ready

Player One imagine vast virtual environments where creativity, identity, and collaboration collide. These spaces matter. But even the most advanced platforms fall short of the spark generated when people meet in the same physical space.

Amazon CEO Andy Jassy once noted that when his teams worked entirely remotely, "We didn't riff the same way." Innovation, he argued, often comes from those unscripted, in-between moments – the corridor chats, the lunch breaks, the spontaneous overlaps.

The Architecture of Ideas

Third places – whether in ancient Athens or modern offices – remind us that creativity is not only about individuals but about environments. They are the architecture of ideas.

And so, the question for leaders and creators alike becomes this: Where are your third places? And how might you design or rediscover circles of trust that help your best ideas come alive?

NATURE AS MUSE:
COLOUR, MOVEMENT, AND ENVIRONMENT

"Only thoughts reached by walking have value."
– Friedrich Nietzsche

The Science of Nature and Creativity

The Genius Loci isn't confined to buildings or city streets. Sometimes the most powerful collaborator in the creative process is the natural world itself. Modern neuroscience is beginning to explain what poets, philosophers, and walkers have always known: nature restores the mind and fuels original thought.

This relationship between rest and creativity came up in my recent SuperCreativity podcast interview with neuroscientist Dr. Joseph Jebelli, author of The Brain at Rest. He spoke about the vital role of the brain's default mode network – the system that activates when we're not focused on a specific task. This network, he explained, is where deeper integration, reflection, and imagination happen.

Jebelli also shares another striking insight: time spent in nature – especially through forest bathing, the Japanese practice of walking mindfully in wooded environments – has been shown to increase creative problem-solving by up to 50%, and improve memory recall by 20%, compared to walking in urban settings. These aren't soft benefits – they're hardwired neurological responses.

Colour matters too. Studies from the University of British Columbia found that the colour blue doubles the number of creative outputs compared with red, while green environments boost divergent thinking and idea generation. Researchers in Berlin and at the University of Exeter have shown that even a few potted plants in a workspace can increase creativity and productivity by 15%, while access to views of nature measurably improves problem-solving ability.

Walking, Water, and the Writer's Mind

Great creators have always tapped into this connection. John le Carré, the celebrated spy novelist, insisted that every one of his books began on foot – through morning jogs and evening walks where storylines and characters would surface unbidden. I often think about his words when I'm out running on Hampstead Heath at the weekends. The rustle of trees, the expanse of sky, the rhythm of moving feet – it is in those moments that ideas I've been wrestling with at my desk suddenly fall into place.

And it's not just anecdotal: a landmark Stanford study found that walking boosts creative output by 60% compared to sitting, proving what writers like le Carré sensed intuitively.

Business leaders also lean on this muse. Mark Zuckerberg often conducts walking meetings around the Menlo Park campus, Jeff Weiner of LinkedIn has spoken about walking as his most productive habit, and Jack Dorsey made early-morning jogs part of his thinking routine. Companies like Amazon and Google design greenery, gardens, and walking paths into their headquarters – not for aesthetics alone, but because movement and nature spark better thinking.

In my own life, I've experienced this repeatedly. While living in Perthshire, Scotland, I noticed how long walks in the glens would unlock solutions to creative blocks that hours at a desk never could. Nature, in this sense, is not just a backdrop to creativity – it is a collaborator. A muse that steadies our minds, sparks imagination, and connects us to something larger than ourselves.

In the end, nature is not just scenery – it is strategy. It clears the noise, refreshes the mind, and invites the kind of breakthroughs that fluorescent lights rarely deliver. So ask yourself: How could you design your days and your workspaces to make nature not an escape from creativity, but a daily partner in it?

Because if nature can act as muse, then the very design of our environments – the flow of space, light, and movement – can become collaborators too. And that takes us to our next exploration: designing for flow.

DESIGNING FOR FLOW

"Within you there is a stillness and a sanctuary to which you can retreat at any time." – Hermann Hesse

The Architecture of Attention

Walk into any workspace and you can almost feel whether creativity is welcome there – or quietly suffocated. Our environments are not neutral. They either amplify our ability to focus, connect, and imagine, or they quietly drain it away. Psychologists call this the architecture of attention. It's the subtle interplay of light, sound, layout, and even temperature that shapes how our minds operate.

Think about the difference between sitting in a sterile, grey cubicle with buzzing fluorescent lights versus a sunlit studio with open windows and greenery. One contracts your imagination. The other expands it. Creativity thrives not in accident but in environments intentionally designed for flow.

What Flow Needs to Flourish

Flow – the state of being fully immersed and energised in your work – doesn't happen by chance. It happens when challenge and skill are in balance, distractions are minimised, and the environment nudges us into deep focus.

Stanford researchers found that open, uncluttered layouts encourage divergent thinking, while small "focus pods" enhance convergent thinking – the narrowing of ideas into solutions. In other words: great creative environments don't privilege one type of thinking. They give you places to expand and places to refine.

This is why LEGO's headquarters in Billund, Denmark, has become a case study in designing for flow. The campus includes tree-lined walking paths, bright play-zones with oversized LEGO bricks, and open staircases that connect teams across floors. Employees move seamlessly from playful collaborative areas into quiet focus rooms. As one executive put it, "We design play into the building because play is how we create."

Rhythm and Ritual

But designing for flow isn't just about architecture, it's also about rhythm. Neuroscience shows that our brains cycle through peaks and troughs of attention roughly every 90 minutes. Great creative environments recognise this and make space for natural rhythms: breakout zones, walking paths, even nap pods.

At LEGO, employees often take "walk and talk" meetings outdoors or use short breaks in the play-areas to reset. These pauses aren't wasted time – they're built-in recovery moments that help sustain creative energy across the day.

In my own work, I've noticed how much faster ideas crystallise when I respect these rhythms. Writing a keynote in the quiet of my study, rehearsing in an open room where I can move, then refining slides in a more focused space – each step is matched to a place that supports it. The right environment reduces friction and lets momentum build.

Mise en Place for Creative Work

The best creative spaces, however, aren't always external. They can also be internal sanctuaries, shaped by routines, rituals, and the arrangement of our tools. Chefs have a concept called mise en place – everything in its place. It's a disciplined setup where every tool and ingredient is within arm's reach, minimising friction and maximising focus. Tailors, surgeons, and designers often adopt similar practices. And so should we.

One of my favourite restaurants is Studio Gauthier in London, created by French chef Alexis Gauthier. It's a fully plant-based restaurant renowned for culinary innovations like vegan "caviar" and even 3Dprinted steaks, with a celebrity following that ranges from Sir Paul McCartney and Tom Cruise to Billie Eilish and David Beckham. What fascinates me most, though, is the quiet choreography of the kitchen: each movement flows because every knife, spoon, and garnish is exactly where it needs to be. That's mise en place in motion.

Your physical environment should support your flow the same way. Cluttered desks and random distractions don't just waste time – they deplete cognitive energy. One surprising source of distraction? Your smartphone. Even when turned off and placed nearby, it draws on your brain's limited resources. Recent research confirms that the mere presence of a mobile phone reduces cognitive capacity and impairs analytical thinking. As Harvard Business Review puts it: "Having your smartphone nearby takes a toll on your thinking."

Designing for creativity means being intentional. Clear your space, organise your tools, and consider what's within reach. What supports your thinking? What silently drains it?

Flow Is Designed, Not Discovered

The myth is that flow arrives when conditions are perfect. The truth is that flow arrives when conditions are designed. From offices to studios to home workspaces, we can shape environments that help ideas move faster, deeper, and further.

So ask yourself: what small changes could you make to the design of your workspace to turn it from a container of work into a catalyst for flow?

Because once you understand how spaces channel focus and energy, you begin to see your environment not as a backdrop but as a partner in the creative process. And that opens the door to our next exploration: how to think differently by changing not just the spaces we're in, but the very temperatures we create – what I call Thermal Thinking.

THERMAL THINKING: HOW TEMPERATURE SHAPES IDEAS

"That's why so many insights happen during warm showers. For many people, it's the most relaxing part of the day." – Joydeep Bhattacharya

The Goldilocks Effect

When people talk about creative environments, they usually mention design, light, or layout. Rarely do they mention temperature. And yet, it might be one of the most overlooked factors in how we think and create. Too hot, and your mind slows, sliding into fatigue. Too cold, and you huddle inward, conserving energy rather than taking risks. Get it just right, and ideas seem to flow.

I've noticed this during the creation of this book. Writing in the depths of a Scottish Highland winter, I often find my creativity shrinks with the cold. The chill makes me more cautious, more analytical. In contrast, when I'm at my vacation home in

Italy – tending to my olive trees or looking at the Renaissance hilltop towns in the distance – I feel sharper, quicker, more willing to improvise and take creative risks. These shifts aren't just about comfort – they're about cognition. Temperature is the silent partner in every brainstorm, boardroom, and breakout session.

The Science of Heat and Focus

Research suggests that creativity thrives between 22°C and 24°C (72°F to 75°F). This range supports a balance between comfort and alertness. But it goes deeper. Warm environments appear to encourage divergent thinking – free-flowing, spontaneous idea generation. Cooler spaces, by contrast, support convergent thinking – focused analysis and decision-making.

Cornell University researchers found that office workers made significantly fewer typing errors when the room temperature was raised from 20°C (68°F) to 25°C (77°F). At cooler temperatures, employees were not only less productive but also more error-prone. A separate study published in Building and Environment reinforced the point: moderate warmth increases creative output, while extremes on either end drain cognitive energy.

Temperature, in other words, doesn't just affect how comfortable you feel – it influences the very style of thinking your brain defaults to.

Cultural Wisdom: Hot Baths and Cold Plunges

Long before scientists measured creativity in degrees Celsius, cultures around the world understood the power of temperature to shift consciousness.

The Romans built their baths not just as places of hygiene but as centres of debate, politics, and philosophy. Ideas flowed as freely as the heated waters. In Scandinavia, the sauna has long been a place for both social bonding and private reflection – followed by the shock of a cold plunge that refreshes body and mind. In Japan, onsens – natural hot springs – are seen as sacred spaces where relaxation and clarity come together.

These traditions recognised something modern neuroscience confirms: changing the body's thermal state changes the mind's state. The shock of hot to cold can jolt the brain into alertness. The warmth of a bath or fire can soften defences, open emotions, and encourage conversation. Temperature, in this sense, becomes an intentional design element for creativity.

Business Lessons: Designing Thermal Zones

Forward-thinking companies are beginning to take note. Rather than standardising the entire office at one static temperature, some are experimenting with thermal zones: cooler areas for focused, detailed work, and warmer, lounge-like areas for brainstorming and collaborative creativity.

Consider how conferences feel different depending on their climate control. I've spoken in ballrooms so cold you could see people hugging themselves, their creative energy shut down by discomfort. Contrast that with venues where the air felt alive, balanced, and comfortable – the kind of atmosphere where participants stayed engaged for hours and ideas kept building. The lesson? Leaders should pay as much attention to thermal design as they do to lighting or acoustics.

Thermal Thinking in My Own Work

I've experienced this contrast vividly in my own career. When I'm in my study in Scotland during the winter, with the log fire burning and the air just cool enough to keep me alert, I find myself focused, precise, sometimes even ruthless in editing. But in Dubai, stepping out of the desert heat into an air-conditioned hall, I feel a different energy altogether – spontaneous, improvisational, quick to connect ideas and weave stories for an audience.

Both climates have their genius loci, their own creative spirits. The Highland cold pushes me to sharpen. The desert warmth invites me to expand. Together, they remind me that creativity isn't only in the mind – it's in the body.

From Comfort to Catalyst

So the question isn't simply, "Am I comfortable?" It's "What kind of thinking does this temperature invite?" If you want precision, maybe lower the thermostat. If you want openness, perhaps raise it a degree or two – or even step outside into the sun.

Temperature, like light or sound, can be intentionally shaped to support the work at hand. It's another tool in the creative leader's kit. The key is to notice, experiment, and design for it.

So ask yourself: How is the temperature of your environment shaping the quality of your ideas today? And if you shifted it – warmer, cooler, or even through the shock of contrast – what new ways of thinking might emerge?

Because once you begin to see thermal thinking as a creative lever, you stop treating temperature as background noise. You start treating it as another collaborator.

And from here, we'll move from how we shape the feel of our environments to how we design their interface – how place itself can become a tool for thinking, not just a container for it.

PLACE AS INTERFACE

"Discovery consists not in seeking new lands, but in seeing with new eyes." – Marcel Proust

The Spirit of Place

As we've discussed, the Romans believed that every place had its own spirit – a genius loci. This wasn't just superstition; it was an acknowledgment that the character of a space, whether an office, factory, studio or laboratory shapes the character of the people within it. A place could elevate you, diminish you, or open you to new ways of seeing. For the Romans, this "spirit of place" was almost like a collaborator – an unseen partner in the work of living, building, and creating.

That idea has never left us. Today, as leaders and creators, we are beginning to rediscover what the ancient Greeks and Romans already knew: place is not neutral. It is not just a backdrop. It is an interface. The environments we inhabit connect us to one another, frame our thinking, and either accelerate or suffocate creativity.

When Place Shapes Breakthroughs

History shows us that the right place can become a crucible of innovation. Florence during the Renaissance wasn't just a city, it was a living interface where artists, architects, scientists, and philosophers collided. The Medici family's patronage mattered, yes, but so did the streets, workshops, and piazzas where painters argued with engineers, and poets shared wine with mathematicians. The Renaissance was born not in isolation, but in proximity.

Bletchley Park during the Second World War functioned the same way. Its collection of huts and manor houses was deliberately filled with mathematicians, linguists, engineers, and codebreakers. It wasn't individual brilliance alone that cracked the Enigma code, but the design of a place where different kinds of minds could work in concert.

Modern Interfaces for Innovation

Today, forward-thinking organisations apply the same principle.

Arup, the global design and engineering firm, embodies this through its culture of "total architecture". Its studios are designed for collisions: architects sit beside acousticians, planners beside structural engineers. By treating the office as a creative interface, Arup has delivered projects from the Sydney Opera House to Beijing's Olympic stadium

SAP has taken a similar approach with its AppHaus network. These co-creation spaces are intentionally playful, colourful, and flexible. They aren't built to impress clients. They're built to invite iteration, mess, and energy. Clients and employees gather shoulder-to-shoulder to prototype, turning abstract problems into tangible solutions.

In Singapore, Fusionopolis and Biopolis form vast ecosystems where labs, offices, and residences intermingle. Scientists walk from their apartments into shared facilities, bump into venture capitalists over coffee, and spend evenings at cultural performances – all within the same complex. Place itself is engineered to shorten the distance between idea and execution.

Place as a Business Tool

What unites these examples is a simple truth: place is not just a container of activity – it is an active force that shapes it. In software design, we talk about the user interface – the layout that determines how humans interact with code. Place functions in the same way. It is the interface through which human creativity is channelled, amplified, or diminished.

Research backs this up. A study in the Journal of Environmental Psychology found that employees in well-designed, activity-based offices reported 31% higher levels of idea generation compared to those in conventional layouts. The genius loci isn't just a poetic idea, it's measurable.

Listening to What Places Whisper

Every place carries signals – subtle cues that tell us how to think, behave, and interact. A sterile cubicle farm whispers "comply". A buzzing studio filled with whiteboards whispers "improvise". A co-creation lab says "experiment".

Leaders who treat place as a cost centre end up with sterile, lifeless environments. Leaders who treat it as an interface create spaces that encourage serendipity, trust, and flow. The art of leadership is listening to those whispers – and designing places that speak clearly.

So ask yourself: do you see your office, studio, or virtual space as a cost – or as an interface? Do you treat it as neutral, or as a collaborator with its own genius loci? And most importantly: do you have the systems, rituals, and designs in place to make your environment a true partner in creativity?

The Next Frontier: Product, Persuasion, and the Power of Human+Machine Creativity

If People are the collaborators and Process is the method, then Place is the stage on which creativity plays out. It is where the genius loci shapes what is possible, where ideas are sparked, tested, and refined. But even the most inspiring places are no longer enough on their own. Increasingly, we find ourselves working with a new kind of collaborator – one that doesn't sit at the table, but powers the table itself: machines.

In the next part of this book, we'll explore Human+Machine creativity – how emerging technologies like AI are changing the way ideas are generated, developed, and scaled. And we'll turn to the final two Ps of this framework: Product (what emerges from all that inner and collective work) and Persuasion (how you convince others to join you, fund you, or follow you).

Because creativity doesn't stop with a spark or a team – it only becomes real when it takes form in the world and earns the belief of others.

Next Actions

Do This Week
1. **Audit Your Creative Spaces**
    Choose three places where you regularly think, write, meet, or plan. For each one, ask: Does this space energize me, distract me, or drain me? Make one small change in one space: declutter, add natural light, change seating, or introduce a plant or colour.
2. **Design a Third Place for Yourself**
    Identify or create a space that isn't home or formal work – your personal "third place". It could be a coffee shop, library corner, bar, garden, or coworking lounge. Use it this week for idea generation, journaling, or informal collaboration.

Download the worksheet for this chapter on Place as well as bonus content at www.supercreativitybook.com

Reflect and Reframe

Questions to Ask Yourself
*   Where do I consistently do my best thinking – and what is it about that space helps me focus or flow?
*   Do the spaces I design (at work or home) invite collaboration and curiosity – or just routine and control?
*   What simple, intentional change could I make today to better support the kind of thinking I need right now – divergent or convergent?

Key Takeaways

SuperCreator's Cheat Sheet
- Place is not passive. Where you think shapes how you think. The best spaces invite focus, flow, or connection – not just convenience.
- Third places matter. Informal, neutral spaces – coffee shops, gardens, creative corners – are powerful catalysts for ideation and collaboration.
- Movement fuels insight. Walking meetings, green spaces, and sensory-rich environments can unlock unexpected breakthroughs.
- Temperature affects cognition. Warmer settings promote expansive thinking; cooler ones support editing and analysis. Tune your environment to match your task.
- Design your creative *mise en place*. Clear clutter, organize tools, and eliminate micro-distractions (like your phone) to preserve cognitive energy.
- Create with intention. Whether you're alone, with a team, or alongside AI, your space is a silent collaborator in the creative process.

PART 3

HUMAN+MACHINE CREATIVITY

"Intelligence is the ability to adapt to change."
– Stephen Hawking

The Human Leap: A Story from the Future

In 2016, millions watched as Lee Sedol, one of the greatest Go players in history, faced off against AlphaGo, an artificial intelligence developed by London based DeepMind.

Go is an ancient Chinese board game, played for more than 2,500 years and considered one of the world's most profound tests of strategy and creativity. The number of potential board positions in Go exceeds the number of atoms in the observable universe. For centuries, it was believed that only human intuition and imagination could navigate its complexity.

AlphaGo proved otherwise. It won. Repeatedly. Until, in game four, Sedol played Move 78 – so surprising and brilliant that experts called it "The God's Touch". Sedol later admitted he might never have discovered it without an artificial intelligence pushing him to the edge of his ability.

That match was more than a contest. It was a preview of our future: a world where creativity emerges not from humans alone, nor machines alone, but from the tension, challenge, and partnership between the two.

From SuperCreativity to SuperCollaboration

Throughout this book we've explored SuperCreativity – the ways purpose, personality, practice, process, people, and place amplify human imagination. But as technology evolves, a new dimension has emerged: SuperCollaboration.

If SuperCreativity asks, "How can creativity be enhanced by connection?" SuperCollaboration asks, "What happens when that connection is with intelligent machines?"

This is not about replacement. It is about partnership. About building high-performing relationships where humans and AI each bring their strengths – intuition and imagination on one side, speed and scale on the other.

Why Human+Machine Collaboration Matters

Three forces make this moment different from any before:

1. **Complexity is increasing.** The challenges we face – from climate change to global supply chains – are too vast for any single mind or team.
2. **Creativity is becoming the ultimate advantage.** As routine tasks are automated, our uniquely human ability to imagine and innovate becomes our edge.
3. **Collaboration itself is evolving.** We are moving from teamwork to *team-tech*: blended groups of humans and machines, creating side by side.

The future of creativity doesn't belong to humans or machines alone. It belongs to those who can work together.

The evidence is compelling. At Boston Consulting Group, consultants who had access to generative AI tools were able to complete twelve-percent more tasks, work twenty-five percent faster, and deliver work judged to be forty-percent higher in quality than their peers who did not use AI. McKinsey projects that the widespread adoption of generative AI could generate between $2.6 and $4.4 trillion in annual value across industries, while PwC goes even further, forecasting a $15.7 trillion boost to the global economy by 2030.

Beyond productivity and growth, the human benefits are equally striking. In a global survey of 10,000 professionals, nearly three-quarters of those using AI tools said they felt more fulfilled and creative in their roles, compared with less than half of those who weren't leveraging the technology. The message is clear: when designed with intention, Human+Machine partnerships do more than improve performance – they also elevate happiness, engagement, and meaning at work.

The Cybernetic Teammate

Another way to win both the hearts and minds of people is by showing them that AI doesn't just improve performance – it can make us happier.

A Harvard Business School working paper titled "The Cybernetic Teammate" explored what happens when humans and AI collaborate in different combinations. The findings were striking:

- A **human team** produces better work than a human working alone.

- An **individual with a team of AIs** produces better work than a team made up only of humans.
- And the highest quality of all? A **human team working with AI teammates**.

But quality wasn't the only factor. The researchers also found that those individuals and teams who worked with AI reported higher levels of happiness, fulfilment, and engagement than those who did not.

This suggests that AI's role is not just about speeding up tasks or raising output. Done right, collaboration with AI actually improves the human experience of work – freeing us from drudgery and helping us focus on the parts of our craft that bring the most meaning.

Centaurs, Cyborgs, and the Rise of SuperCollaborative Teams

In the same study, two groups of participants consistently outperformed the rest.

The first – termed Cyborgs – worked in deep integration with the AI. They didn't just use the machine occasionally; they intertwined with it. Cyborgs constantly moulded, checked, and refined its outputs, treating the AI as an extension of their own thinking. It reminds me of my father, a jazz guitarist, whose guitar became more than an instrument – it was an extension of his mind, body and soul.

The second group – called Centaurs – took a different approach. Like the mythological creature with the body of a horse and the head of a human, Centaurs divided the labour strategically. They delegated subtasks to the AI – research, drafting, analysis – while focusing their own energy on the aspects requiring human judgment, creativity, and intuition.

Both models worked. What mattered wasn't the exact strategy, but the intentionality. The top performers weren't those who ignored the AI, nor those who blindly trusted it. They were the ones who consciously designed a way of working with it – whether as a tightly integrated partner (Cyborg) or as a powerful collaborator handling specific tasks (Centaur).

And this is where the future points us. Leaders will need to decide: Do we want our people working as Centaurs, using AI selectively to free up their uniquely human strengths? Or do we want them as Cyborgs, embedding AI into every step of their process? The answer may depend on context. Centaur models may suit areas like law, medicine, or consulting, where judgment and ethics are paramount, while Cyborg models may thrive in design, R&D, and storytelling, where iteration and speed create breakthroughs.

Some organisations will go even further, forming SuperCollaborative Teams – groups of humans and AIs collaborating at scale, each member augmenting the others. In these settings, creativity becomes less about lone individuals and more about orchestrating the dance between human imagination and machine intelligence.

Centaurs, Cyborgs, and SuperCollaborative Teams aren't just metaphors. They are choices – choices about identity, workflow, and culture. And the leaders who make these choices consciously will shape the creative frontier of the Human+Machine era.

Why We Now Turn to Product and Persuasion

In Parts 1 and 2, we explored the foundations of creativity: purpose, personality, practice, process, people, and place. These shaped the conditions for SuperCreativity.

Now, in Part 3, we turn to the outputs – the places where imagination meets impact:

- **Product – What are you creating?**
- **Persuasion – Who needs convincing?**

These are the outward expressions of creativity. And they are also the two areas where SuperCollaboration – the partnership between humans and machines – is already driving the most profound change.

In Product, AI is transforming how we generate ideas, prototype, test, and scale. In Persuasion, AI is reshaping how we tell stories, communicate value, and inspire action.

Together, they form the new frontier of Human+Machine creativity. This is where imagination turns into execution – and where your next big idea becomes real.

CHAPTER 7

PRODUCT (WHAT WE CREATE)

"If you are not embarrassed by the first version of your product, you've launched too late." – Reid Hoffman

Pizza, Pompeii, and Pineapple

In early 2023, archaeologists made a discovery in Pompeii that stirred more than just academic interest. On the wall of a Roman house with an attached bakery, they uncovered a fresco that looked uncannily like a pizza.

Of course, it wasn't the pizza we order today. Tomatoes, brought from the Americas centuries later, were nowhere to be found. Cheese, as we know it, was missing too. Instead, the fresco showed a flatbread topped with fruit, oil, and spices. But one topping caught everyone's attention: something that looked suspiciously like pineapple.

Yes, there's a chance that the first "Hawaiian pizza" predates Hawaii by nearly two thousand years. Which means that food debates, like whether pineapple belongs on pizza, may be even older than we thought.

It's a charming story, but it carries a larger point. Human beings have always been makers, and what we make has always been shaped by the tools available to us. For the Romans, those tools included ovens, milling stones, and spice routes. Fast-forward two millennia, and our kitchens no longer rely on volcanic stone but on algorithms, sensors, and machine-learning models.

The act of creation has always been a conversation between human imagination and technological possibility. And just as the flatbread fresco reminds us how ingredients evolve, today's products – from food to finance to pharmaceuticals – are being reinvented by a new ingredient: artificial intelligence.

Algorithmic Kitchens and SuperCollaboration

If pizza shows us how long the human appetite for reinvention has lasted, today's food industry reveals how radically our methods are changing. Consider Climax Foods, a California startup founded by astrophysicist and former Google/SpaceX researcher Oliver Zahn.

Climax is reimagining cheese. Not by trying to mimic dairy, but by out-innovating it. Their approach, called precision formulation, is a data-driven, machine-learning–powered method of food development. Instead of asking, "How can we copy cheese?" Climax asks, "How can we create something that performs even better?"

Here's how it works. Their system analyses up to 300,000 different plant-based ingredients – everything from legumes to seeds – scanning for variables like taste, texture, meltability, nutrition, and cost. The AI handles the heavy lifting, generating thousands of possible formulations and simulating how each would perform. Then the humans step in: chefs and food scientists taste, tweak, and decide which prototypes move forward.

This loop of human judgment and machine exploration is where the magic happens. On their own, the scientists could never manually test 300,000 options. On its own, the AI would never know which flavour feels indulgent or comforting. But together, they're developing plant-based cheeses that don't just pass for dairy – in some cases, they surpass it in stretch, melt, and mouthfeel.

What once took years of trial-and-error in food labs can now be compressed into weeks. And this isn't limited to niche start-ups. Major companies like The Bel Group – makers of Babybel and Boursin – are already working with Climax to reinvent entire product lines.

The lesson? It's not "human versus machine". It's human with machine.

This is what I call SuperCollaboration: the fusion of human creativity and curiosity with machine precision, speed, and scale to increase productivity and drive innovation. It's not about replacing the human spark, but about amplifying it – building things together that neither could make alone.

Beyond Food: The Universal Pattern

While Climax Foods makes for a delicious example, this pattern is repeating across industries. Airbus uses AI to generate thousands of possible designs for aircraft panels and overhead bins, which engineers then evaluate for strength, weight, and efficiency. Law firms now lean on AI systems to review contracts in seconds, spotting risks that human lawyers might miss after hours of work. Architects feed design goals into generative systems that produce forms no single human mind would imagine. In every case, the workflow is the same:

1. **Humans set the intent.** What problem are we solving? What constraints matter most?

2. **Machines generate possibilities.** Thousands of options, permutations, or drafts.
3. **Humans curate and refine.** Selecting, editing, and shaping the outputs.
4. **Together, they create something new.**

This is the Human+Machine Co-Creation Loop. It's not science fiction – it's happening in boardrooms, studios, and factories today.

From Pizza to Products of the Future

The story of Pompeii's pineapple pizza reminds us that making has always been a blend of necessity, creativity, and experimentation. But unlike the Romans, we now have collaborators that don't sleep, don't tire, and can generate thousands of ideas in the time it takes us to sketch one.

The question for modern creators isn't "Will AI replace us?" but rather:

- When do we lean on instinct, and when do we rely on data?
- When do we go wide and explore, and when do we narrow down and refine?
- How do we ensure that what we create is not only new, but also meaningful?

These are the creative tensions every maker now faces. They aren't problems to solve, but dynamics to navigate. And the best creators of tomorrow will be those who know how to move fluidly between them.

Which brings us to the heart of this chapter: the three tensions shaping how products are made in the age of SuperCollaboration.

The Three Creative Tensions

To answer the question of what we're really creating in this new era of SuperCollaboration, we need to talk about tensions again.

Every maker and creative using AI today now face three fundamental creative tensions:

1. **Risk vs. Certainty**
2. **Exploration vs. Refinement**
3. **Novelty vs. Meaningfulness**

These tensions aren't problems to solve once and for all. They're dynamics to navigate. And the best creators – today and tomorrow – will be the ones who know how to move fluidly between them.

Creative Tension No. 1: Risk vs. Certainty

> *"If you're not prepared to be wrong, you'll never come up with anything original."* – Sir Ken Robinson

When do we trust instinct, and when do we trust the AI model?

The British design theorist David Pye made a distinction that every modern creator should know by heart: the difference between the workmanship of risk and the workmanship of certainty.

- The **workmanship of certainty** is about control. The process is tightly defined, the outcome almost guaranteed. Think injection-moulded plastic. Think an assembly line. Or today, think of an AI cranking out 10,000 product descriptions in a few minutes. It's efficient, measurable, and repeatable. The machine does what it was told.

- The **workmanship of risk** is about feel. The outcome isn't guaranteed, because the craftsperson is making decisions in the moment. It's the hand-thrown pot, the live jazz solo, the product designer trusting her gut over the focus group. It's where true creativity – and all its glorious uncertainty – lives.

What makes this moment so fascinating is that we no longer have to choose. We can now move between both.

Take Doug Dietz, the industrial designer at GE Healthcare. Dietz had helped design a next-generation MRI scanner. Technically, it was a masterpiece: beautifully engineered, functionally flawless. The epitome of certainty.

Until the day he saw a young boy walk into the scanning room, take one look at the machine, and burst into tears.

The product worked. But to a child, it looked like a torture device.

Instead of shrugging, Dietz took a risk. He and his team re-imagined the whole experience. They turned the MRI scanners into pirate ships and spacecrafts. They trained technicians to tell stories. The machine didn't change. But the children's experience did. Sedation rates plummeted. Smiles skyrocketed.

SuperCollaboration isn't about picking risk or certainty, it's about knowing when to simulate and when to improvise.

Creative Tension No. 2: Exploration vs. Refinement

"The essence of strategy is choosing what not to do."
– Michael Porter

When do we go wide, and when do we go deep?

Every act of creativity is a dance between opening and closing – between generating possibilities and narrowing them down.

In creativity research, this is often described as the balance between divergent thinking (exploring many ideas) and convergent thinking (selecting and shaping the best ones). Divergence gets the glory, but convergence – the act of choosing – turns potential into product.

And this is where AI changes the rhythm.

AI accelerates divergence. It can generate hundreds of options in seconds. What it can't do – at least not well – is decide which ones matter most.

Consider food again. 3D-printed food may sound like a gimmick, but it's quickly becoming a proving ground for how AI can expand exploration while still requiring human refinement.

At Steakholder Foods, scientists are printing Wagyu beef using lab-grown tissue. At Columbia University, researchers have developed ways to 3D-print entire desserts – cheesecakes layered with precision that no pastry chef could achieve. Hershey has even experimented with custom-printed chocolates.

These aren't stunts. They're the prototypes of a new food logic, where form, flavour, and function can be programmed, iterated, and evolved.

But despite the engineering wizardry, no algorithm can decide whether a cheesecake feels right on the tongue, or whether a chocolate bar carries the emotional comfort of childhood. AI can generate the recipes. Humans still choose the winners.

You can see the same pattern in the digital world. Google's Duet AI now offers an "Attend for You" option which can send a Digital Twin of you to the meeting on your behalf. Your Digital Twin knows much of what you do and will ask many of the questions it knows you would be likely to ask. It can summarise meetings, draft emails, even suggest strategies based on past behaviour. It's brilliant for widening the field of input – surfacing patterns and possibilities you might have missed. But would you trust it to write your next big presentation? Not yet.

What's emerging is a new kind of rhythm in the creative process:

- Humans define the intent.
- AI explores the terrain.
- Humans decide what to pursue.
- AI helps polish and scale.
- Humans add the final touch.

The human role becomes that of creative director. The AI is the co-brainstormer, the co-writer, the collaborator. But the human still brings discernment.

The skill isn't just generating more ideas. It's having the courage to choose.

Creative Tension No. 3: Novelty vs. Meaningfulness

"There is no greatness where there is no simplicity, goodness, and truth." – Leo Tolstoy

Just because we can create something doesn't mean we should.

Novelty on its own isn't enough. In The Cambridge Handbook of Creativity, Kaufman and Sternberg define a creative product as one that is both novel and appropriate. It must be original, yes, but also useful, relevant, or meaningful.

Without usefulness, creativity becomes chaos. Without novelty, it becomes repetition.

Take Cera Care, the UK-based home health platform. They weren't chasing novelty for its own sake. They wanted to keep elderly patients out of hospital. By analysing care notes from over 10,000 carers, their AI could spot subtle patterns that humans missed – predicting hospitalisations up to 30 times faster than traditional systems. That's not just new. That's meaningful.

Or consider SoftVoice, a technology designed to protect call-centre workers. By filtering out abusive language in real-time, the AI prevents human agents from having to listen to toxic speech. A small innovation, but one that makes life better for the call centre worker.

These are reminders that the true test of a product is not whether it is clever, but whether it makes life better of us, the humans.

The best question a modern maker can ask isn't "Can we build this?" but "Should we?"

Navigating the Tensions

These three tensions – Risk vs. Certainty, Exploration vs. Refinement, Novelty vs. Meaningfulness – aren't problems to be solved. They're forces to be balanced.

AI doesn't dissolve them. It sharpens them. And the best creators will be those who learn to move between them like musicians shifting keys: sometimes following the score, sometimes improvising.

THE LIVING PRODUCT AND AGENTIC AI

"What we call the beginning is often the end. And to make an end is to make a beginning." – T.S. Eliot

The Rise of Living Products

Once upon a time, products were fixed. You designed them, built them, shipped them, and maybe – if you were lucky – you released version 2.0 the following year. That rhythm now feels prehistoric.

Today, products don't just launch – they learn. They adapt to how we use them, when we abandon them, and what frustrates us. Increasingly, they don't just respond – they anticipate.

This is the rise of what I call the living product: something that continues to evolve long after it leaves the hands of its original creator.

Consider any of the Generative AI tools like ChatGPT or CoPilot. At first glance, they look like a supercharged assistant: they can draft emails, take meeting notes, and even suggest strategies in real time. But look closer and you see something more: a system that adapts to your personal style, reflects your preferences, and grows with you. They are less like static tools and more like creative proxies – ones that evolve alongside your work.

At Zillow, AI development runs along two tracks. The Red Team focuses on optimisation – making valuations more accurate, searches faster, and the buying process smoother. The Blue Team pushes innovation, experimenting with new features that can change the marketplace.

One Blue Team breakthrough was virtual staging. Instead of physically furnishing a property for photos, agents can now upload empty room images and, within seconds, AI generates hyper-realistic interiors in styles from "mid-century modern" to "Art Deco with pink accents". Zillow is integrating this into its listing platform, saving sellers time and cost while giving buyers a more compelling vision of a home's potential.

Together, the Red Team's refinements and the Blue Team's experiments make Zillow a living product – constantly improving, constantly evolving.

Even healthcare is seeing this shift. Take Cera Care, which we met earlier. Their predictive AI doesn't stop learning once it's deployed. Every new carer note makes the system more precise at spotting early signs of patient decline. The product evolves with the people it serves.

And it's not just software. Cars today are, in many ways, living products. They receive over-the-air updates that adjust everything from battery performance to user interface to driver assistance. Owners wake up to find their vehicle has new capabilities – sometimes features they never imagined when they bought it. You're not purchasing a frozen product; you're entering into an ongoing relationship.

From Tools to Teammates

What ties these stories together is the emergence of Agentic AI – systems that don't just wait for instructions, but show initiative. They exhibit four core behaviours that once felt uniquely human:

- **Autonomy** – They can act without being told exactly what to do.

- **Planning** – They sequence actions over time toward a goal.
- **Tool use** – They can leverage other tools or systems to get work done.
- **Reflection** – They can evaluate outcomes and adjust their own behaviour.

This makes them fundamentally different from the previous generations of AI and automation.

- **Automation** (think assembly lines, RPA bots, or basic algorithms) is about rigid rules: "If X happens, do Y." It is powerful but inflexible.
- **Traditional AI** (think predictive models or recommendation engines) adds adaptability. It can find patterns in data and make predictions, but it still needs human direction for every step.
- **Agentic AI**, by contrast, can *pursue goals*. It doesn't just respond to commands, it figures out *how* to achieve an outcome, chaining actions together, calling other tools, and learning from its own results.

In short: automation executes tasks, traditional AI predicts outcomes, but Agentic AI collaborates. It behaves like a teammate – one that can improvise, adapt, and even surprise you.

Why Agentic AI Matters for SuperCollaboration

This shift matters because creativity is rarely about a single task. It's about navigating ambiguity, moving between exploration and refinement, balancing novelty and meaning.

Earlier generations of AI could only support parts of the process: speeding up research, suggesting options, optimising logistics. Helpful, yes. But they weren't creative collaborators. Agentic AI changes that. It can:

- **Co-explore with you.** Instead of just generating outputs, it can run experiments in parallel, test variations, and report back what worked.
- **Extend your reach.** It can take an idea and autonomously push it into prototypes, run simulations, or call APIs to gather new data.
- **Adapt to your style.** Over time, it can learn your preferences and refine its creative contributions to fit your voice, brand, or taste.
- **Challenge your thinking.** Because it reflects and adjusts, it can suggest alternatives you may not have considered – acting almost like a sparring partner.

As Sam Altman put it in a 2023 talk at Howard University:

If you think of a world where every one of us has a whole company worth of AI assistants that are doing tasks for us to help us express our vision and make things for other people and make these new things in the world… the most important thing then will be the quality of the ideas, the curation of the ideas, because AI can generate lots of ideas, but you still need a human to say, "This is the thing people want." And also humans really care about the human behind something.

That's the essence of SuperCollaboration. The future isn't man versus machine. It's humans collaborating with both human and AI teammates – generating, testing, refining – while still relying on human judgment, taste, and values to decide what matters.

Designing for Change, Not Control

If your product continues to evolve after it leaves your hands, what does that mean for the act of creation? If a service is co-created through Human+Machine collaboration who actually created it? Might AI actually be the new "hidden figures" and "backstage heroes" that allow us humans to take centre stage?

In the industrial era, the goal was stability: ship the car, the appliance, the software, and keep it consistent. In the age of living products, the goal is adaptability: to launch not a finished thing, but a relationship – one that requires updating, tuning, and yes, teaching.

That is a very different kind of creativity. It's less about chiselling a final masterpiece and more about orchestrating systems that will continue to adapt and grow.

And that's not the end of creativity. It's the beginning of a new kind.

FROM MAKER TO ORCHESTRATOR

"A product is never just a product. It's a promise, a signal, a story." – Seth Godin

What are you really making?

Let's return one last time to that Roman fresco in Pompeii. Whether it was the world's first pineapple pizza or simply a flatbread with ambition, someone imagined it, made it, and thought it worthy of preserving on a wall. That's what a product is: an idea turned real. A signal to the future that says, "This is what we thought mattered."

But in the age of SuperCollaboration, the act of making has changed. We are no longer solitary makers chiselling out final forms. We are orchestrators – directing networks of humans and intelligent machines.

- We are shaping products that evolve.
- We are directing tools that think.
- We are collaborating with systems that surprise us.

The 3M Model of Human+Machine Creation

Across industries, this orchestration follows a simple rhythm – what I call the 3M Model:

1. **Map** – Humans frame the challenge while AI scans the landscape, surfacing hidden possibilities.
2. **Make** – AI generates prototypes, designs, or options; humans refine, curate, and shape them into form.
3. **Multiply** – The most meaningful solutions are scaled, automated, and amplified by human purpose.

This is no longer a straight line but a loop – mapping, making, multiplying, then mapping again. Orchestrators know how to keep this cycle moving.

AlphaFold: Orchestrating the Protein Universe

One of the most extraordinary examples of this orchestration is AlphaFold, the breakthrough from Google DeepMind and the same company behind the AlphaGo AI programme mentioned earlier.

For half a century, scientists struggled to predict how proteins fold into 3D shapes. Proteins are the engines of biology, and their structures determine their function. Solving this puzzle was essential to drug discovery, agriculture, and curing disease. But the possibilities were almost infinite – far beyond human capacity to map.

DeepMind's AI cracked the code. AlphaFold predicted more than 200 million protein structures – essentially the entire protein universe. A task once thought to take decades was completed in months.

But AlphaFold was not machine-only or human-only. It was orchestration. Human scientists provided the questions, the vision, and the judgment. AI provided the scale, the speed, and the reach. Together they produced a breakthrough that neither could have achieved alone.

The implications are civilisation-scale: faster cures for disease, stronger crops for food security, entirely new frontiers in bioengineering. This is SuperCollaboration at its highest stakes.

A Walk Between Worlds

This is not an abstract idea for me. On my way to the British Library in London, I often pass DeepMind's offices in King's Cross.

On one side of the street: researchers and engineers training AI systems to tackle proteins, climate, mathematics. On the other: the British Library, home to da Vinci's notebooks, Shakespeare's First Folio, and centuries of human imagination.

It feels like walking between two great libraries – one of the past, filled with the handwritten sparks of history's creative minds, and one of the future, where humans and machines are co-authoring the next chapter.

The message is clear: the role of the creator is shifting. We are no longer just makers. We are orchestrators – moving between imagination and implementation, meaning and novelty, risk and certainty, human insight and machine scale.

And yet, even the most remarkable product isn't enough on its own. It still needs one final ingredient: belief.

Someone has to care. Someone has to try it, buy it, share it, champion it. Products don't spread simply because they exist. They spread because someone is brave enough to stand behind them.

That's the last creative act: persuasion.

Because ideas don't succeed just because they're brilliant. They succeed because humans – not machines – choose to champion them.

And that is where we go next.

Next Actions

Do This Week

1. **Audit Your Product Pipeline** – Review your current projects. Where can AI accelerate mapping options, generating prototypes, or scaling solutions? Flag one opportunity this quarter.

2. **Balance the Tensions** – In your next strategy meeting, explicitly ask: Are we optimising for certainty or taking the right risks? Are we exploring enough before refining? Are we chasing novelty, or ensuring meaning?

3. **Appoint an Orchestrator** – Identify someone (or step into the role yourself) to guide Human+Machine collaboration, ensuring AI is not just a tool but a creative partner.

Download the worksheet for this chapter on Product as well as bonus content at www.supercreativitybook.com

Reflect and Reframe

Questions to Ask Yourself

1. If AI could give you a "whole company of assistants", what would you ask them to work on first – and what would you *never* delegate?
2. How do you currently balance the Three Tensions in your business? Where is your blind spot?
3. Think of AlphaFold compressing decades of discovery into months. What's the "protein-folding problem" in your industry – the complex challenge where Human+Machine orchestration could deliver a step-change breakthrough?

Key Takeaways

SuperCreator's Cheat Sheet

- **3M Model** → *Map* → *Make* → *Multiply.*
- **Three Tensions** → Risk vs. Certainty | Exploration vs. Refinement | Novelty vs. Meaningfulness.
- **Living Products** → Products are never finished; they evolve with feedback and AI updates.
- **Agentic AI** → Beyond automation: AI that plans, adapts, and co-creates with you.
- **AlphaFold Lesson** → Human vision + AI scale = civilisation-level breakthroughs.
- **Your Role** → Not just maker. **Orchestrator.** Direct the loop, design for change, ensure the human signature.

CHAPTER 8

PERSUASION (WHO NEEDS CONVINCING)

"The most powerful person in the world is the storyteller. The storyteller sets the vision, values and agenda of an entire generation that is to come." – Steve Jobs

Here's an uncomfortable truth: a brilliant idea, beautifully connected in your own mind, doesn't matter until you can connect it to others.

That is the second half of creativity: persuasion.

Creativity sparks the idea. Persuasion carries it across the bridge into the world. Without it, the best inventions, the boldest visions, the most elegant solutions remain trapped in notebooks, labs, or slide decks. Potential unrealised.

And you've probably felt this yourself. You've had a great idea – a smarter way of doing things, a product that could save money, a vision that could inspire your team – only to watch it stall because others couldn't see what you saw. The frustration of not being heard. The disappointment of watching an opportunity slip away, not because the idea was weak, but because the persuasion was. That gap – between knowing and convincing – is where so many good ideas go to die.

Think about Microsoft CEO Satya Nadella, standing on stage to announce a new wave of product innovations. The technical breakthroughs behind those products were extraordinary. But the real power lay in Nadella's ability to tell a story about how they fit into people's lives, how they would empower organisations, how they could change the world of work.

Or consider historian Yuval Noah Harari. His TED Talks and bestselling books don't just present facts; they persuade us to see history as story, to view the future as something we have agency over. The brilliance isn't in the data – it's in how he frames it to move minds.

This is the hidden truth: ideas don't succeed just because they're brilliant. They succeed because they're believed.

And in the age of AI, this truth has never been more important. Machines can generate endless ideas, drafts, and pitches. They can flood inboxes and feeds with outputs. But what they cannot do is believe. They cannot stand in front of a sceptical room and say, "This matters – and it should matter to you."

That final act still belongs to us. AI may help us analyse an audience, generate options, or polish delivery, but only humans can decide which idea is worth fighting for – and carry the conviction to make others care.

That's why persuasion is not an optional skill. It is the second half of creativity. It is how imagination becomes impact. And in the chapters ahead, we'll explore the frameworks and stories that can help you do it with clarity, confidence, and courage.

THE 4P PERSUASION FRAMEWORK

"If you want to build a ship, don't drum up people to collect wood... instead, teach them to long for the endless immensity of the sea." – Antoine de Saint-Exupéry

Most people make the mistake of thinking that persuasion starts with their idea.

It doesn't.

It starts with your audience's worldview.

If you want people to say "yes" – to your product, your proposal, your pitch – you have to build a bridge from where they are now to where you want them to go. That journey requires emotional intelligence, narrative structure, and clarity of intent. One of the most effective tools I've found for building that bridge is the 4P Framework.

This simple but powerful structure works whether you're pitching a new idea to the board, making a business case to your manager, or shaping a keynote to move thousands. It moves people from awareness, to urgency, to belief, to action.

Let's walk through it step by step.

1. Position

Start with what your audience already knows – and agrees with.

This is your credibility moment. You earn attention by naming the current state in a way that feels familiar and true. It's like saying, "We're on the same page." You're not pushing. You're aligning.

- **Example 1 (Tech leadership pitch):**
  "We've grown 20% year on year, and our systems have scaled impressively to handle that growth."

- **Example 2 (Creative director to CMO):**
  "We all know the brand refresh is overdue. Customers are confused. Internally, we're not aligned on tone."

Why it works: People don't listen when they feel challenged. They listen when they feel heard. Position earns you that listening.

2. Problem

Next, you introduce the tension – but not just any tension.

This is where you wake people up. You highlight what's broken, what's risky, or what's no longer working. And here's the trick: the most powerful move is to reveal that what they thought was the problem isn't actually the real problem at all.

You reframe the stakes. And when you do, you grab their full attention.

- **Example 1 (Internal innovation pitch):**
  "But that growth is coming at a cost. Our product teams are stretched thin. Engineering velocity has slowed. And our last three launches all missed internal KPIs. We think we have a scaling problem – but what we really have is a collaboration problem."
- **Example 2 (Sustainability team presenting to Chief Data Officer):**
  "We keep asking for better ESG reporting. But the real problem is upstream: we have no standardised supplier data. If we can't see it, we can't change it."

Why it works: People are more open to new ideas when their assumptions are gently but clearly challenged. By redefining the problem, you redefine the kind of change that's needed.

3. Possibilities

Now it's time to raise their sights.

Once the problem is clear – and ideally reframed – you open the door to a better future. This is the moment where the tone shifts from concern to optimism. You paint a picture of what could be, then ground that vision in real-world proof.

Think of this as your "I have a dream" moment. Maybe not in tone, but in structure: you point to a horizon that feels inspiring and attainable.

- **Example 1 (AI transformation lead):**
  "Imagine if teams could experiment with new ideas – without waiting weeks for approvals or integration. That's what Amazon did with its internal "two-pizza teams". Autonomy, paired with accountability. And it scaled."
- **Example 2 (Experience designer):**
  "What if our mobile onboarding could be as intuitive as Duolingo or as personal as Monzo? We know it's possible. Other companies have done it – and they've seen three times the retention within 30 days."

Why it works: Possibility opens the emotional door. Proof walks them through it. You're combining aspiration with evidence.

4. Proposal

Finally, you make the ask – clear, credible, and actionable.

By now, it doesn't feel like a hard sell. It feels like the obvious next step. Your proposal should be simple, realistic, and tied directly to the vision you just outlined.

- **Example 1 (Chief Learning Officer):**
  "That's why I'm proposing we launch a six-month pilot

with 300 learners across three business units. Let's gather data, iterate, and reassess at Q3."

- **Example 2 (Startup founder):**
  "We're raising £2 million to move from R&D to growth – with clear benchmarks on customer acquisition, retention, and platform stability."

Why it works: A strong proposal answers the unspoken question: What do you want me to do next? It gives your audience something concrete to say yes to.

Why the 4Ps Work

The 4P Framework mirrors how humans naturally process persuasive stories:

- We begin with clarity (*Ground me*).
- We feel the stakes (*Wake me up*).
- We glimpse a better outcome (*Inspire me*).
- And then we're guided to action (*Lead me*).

I've seen this structure transform corporate town halls, investor decks, innovation pitches, and international keynotes. It works across industries and cultures because it mirrors human logic and emotional rhythm.

And in today's world of AI-generated decks and endless content, structure is more valuable than ever. Machines can flood the zone with information. But only a human can take that flood and shape it into a narrative that earns attention, builds trust, and moves people to act.

Whether you're convincing a client to take a creative risk, persuading your CFO to fund an internal platform, or rallying your team behind a bold vision, the 4P Framework gives your message structure, soul, and strength.

The 4P Framework gives you the skeleton of persuasion – the essential story arc that takes people from where they are to where you want them to go. But structure alone isn't enough. High-stakes persuasion, whether in the boardroom or on stage, also demands a living process: a way to deeply understand your audience, shape a message that feels made for them, refine it through iteration, and then deliver it with impact.

And this is where things get truly exciting. Because today, AI doesn't just generate slides or talking points – it can amplify your ability to persuade. It can surface hidden insights about the people you need to convince, help you test and sharpen your story, and free you to focus on the one thing only a human can bring: conviction. In the next sub-chapter, we'll explore how to harness this new power through what I call the Taylor-Made Persuasion Loop – Human+Machine process designed to help your best ideas finally break through.

TAYLOR-MADE PRESENTATIONS

"Change happens not by telling people what to do,
but by telling them a story they can see themselves in."
– Brené Brown

The Taylor-Made Method for Moving Minds

The ballroom was heavy with power.

In the front row sat government ministers and dignitaries in traditional Middle Eastern dress – crisp white dishdashas and thawbs, black-and-gold bisht cloaks, and women in flowing abayas. Behind them, the company's executive committee filled the seats in tailored dark suits. Regulators clustered near the back. Partners, senior management and consultants lined the aisles, murmuring in low voices as the lights dimmed.

The family-owned company was one of the region's giants – energy, chemicals, IT, and real estate. Together, these businesses had made them a powerhouse across the Middle East, and now they had asked me to help guide their next transformation.

The newly appointed CEO had called me in for one reason: change. He wanted stories that could stir belief. Global examples that would prove agility and innovation were not luxuries but necessities. And above all, he wanted his people to see that adopting artificial intelligence wasn't a choice for someday – it was a decision for now.

I knew the stakes. If my message landed, it could shift the company's trajectory for years to come. If it didn't, the entire initiative might stall before it ever began.

In the past, I might have relied solely on my research, a few discovery calls, and my intuition about what this kind of audience cared about. But this time, I had help. AI tools analysed psychometric data about the audience, mapped the language and corporate culture their used in recent reports and interviews with key executives, and surfaced the values and concerns that truly drove their decisions. Other tools helped me stress-test different narratives, showing which versions would resonate more strongly with risk-averse CFOs and regulators versus innovation-hungry CTOs and investors.

The result? By the time I walked on stage, I wasn't just giving a keynote. I was giving their keynote – a talk designed for their worldview, their anxieties, their ambitions. And that's the essence of persuasion: not broadcasting an idea, but tailoring it so precisely that the audience feels, "This was made for me."

That's why I call it the Taylor-Made Persuasion Loop. It's a process that blends human creativity and empathy with AI's ability to analyse, iterate, and refine – ensuring your message doesn't just inform, but transforms. And it's not just for professional speakers. Whether you're a senior manager presenting to your executive committee, a department head pitching for resources, or a CEO sharing vision at a town hall, this process will help you persuade with greater impact.

Because persuasion moments aren't always about the big stage. Sometimes they happen in the boardroom, in front of your leadership peers, or across a video call where a decision is on the line. The stakes may feel different, but the need is the same: clarity, confidence, and connection.

Just think of:

- **Mary Barra**, CEO of General Motors, standing before employees to announce the company's all-electric future. It wasn't just an external PR statement – it was an internal persuasion moment, galvanising thousands of managers and engineers to believe in a bold strategic shift.

- Or **Indra Nooyi**, former CEO of PepsiCo, persuading investors, employees, and regulators to back her "Performance with Purpose" strategy. Her challenge wasn't just about launching healthier products – it was convincing multiple stakeholders that PepsiCo could deliver strong financial returns while shifting towards a more sustainable and socially responsible future.

Neither moment was about dazzling the audience. They were about aligning stakeholders, winning trust, and moving people to act. That's the reality of persuasion most leaders face.

So how do you prepare for those moments? For me, it comes down to a nine-step process – a persuasion loop that I've developed as a speaker, consultant, and coach. It's a loop you can use whether you're talking to five executives behind closed doors or 5,000 employees on a livestream.

Step 1: Understand the Audience (AI + Empathy)

The first step in persuasion is to stop talking – and start listening.

Before I design a presentation, I use AI tools to profile my audience. Whether it's a Zoom call with a telecoms CEO who is thinking of inviting me to speak, a conference room of marketing professionals, or an internal leadership team's offsite event, I feed relevant data (interviews, social posts, call transcripts, company reports) into platforms like OpenAI's ChatGPT, Anthropic's Claude, or Google's Gemini.

These Generative AI tools help me understand:

- **Audience personality types** (analytical or empathetic? risk-averse or adventurous?)
- **Decision drivers** (trust? innovation? order?)
- **Communication style** (do they respond better to bold vision or grounded numbers?)

When I spoke to 500 software engineers and project managers in Sorrento, AI showed me the audience valued data, storytelling, and creative thinking. I leaned into metaphor and slightly tech-geek humour. When I worked with a group of lawyers in Germany, the analysis told a different story: they valued order, precision, and logic. So I adjusted my message accordingly knowing that everything that came out of my mouth had to be supported by evidence.

AI gives you precision. Empathy – knowing how your audience thinks and what they value – makes it land.

Step 2: The Tailoring Call – The Human Brief

Next comes what I call the "first fitting". A call with the organiser or decision-maker, designed to uncover emotional and strategic objectives.

Key questions I ask:

- "What would make you say, "That was the best presentation we've ever had"?"
- "How do you want the audience to feel immediately after, and three months later?"
- "What's changed recently that your people haven't yet adapted to?"

For you, it might mean asking your CFO before a budget meeting: What pressure are our people under this quarter? Or checking with HR before a town hall: What's the emotional temperature of the workforce right now?

Persuasion starts not with what you want to say – but with what they need to hear.

Step 3: Message Design with the 4P Framework

Armed with insight, I build the narrative using the 4Ps: Position, Problem, Possibilities, Proposal. For a 30-minute talk, I'll map out 20 cue cards – five per P.

- **Position:** Establish shared reality.
- **Problem:** Reveal the hidden challenge (ideally, reframe it).
- **Possibilities:** Paint the picture, then show who's already done it.

- **Proposal:** Offer a clear, credible next step.

This works just as well for an internal product roadmap update as it does for a keynote. Why? Because it's the natural rhythm of persuasion.

Step 4: Story Selection – Head, Heart, Gut

To resonate, I select three stories:
- One for **logic** (head).
- One for **emotion** (heart).
- One for **instinct** (gut).

The balance ensures different types of thinkers stay engaged. For example:
- A **surprise piece of data** to prove ROI.
- An inspiring **customer study** to show impact.
- An unexpected **underdog story** to spark belief.

Stories don't just illustrate the point. They make people feel the point.

Step 5: Drafting with AI Feedback Loops

With the stories and structure in place, I draft the core message and design the visuals. Then I feed the draft presentation into AI, which overlays audience psychometrics against my content to check:
- Does this presentation, pitch, or keynote match the audience's priorities?
- Am I hitting the right trust signals?
- Does the tone fit their appetite for urgency, detail, or vision?

It's like having a rehearsal partner that never gets tired – helping me spot blind spots before they show up in the room.

Step 6: Design for Visual Impact

Slides should be memory anchors, not wallpaper.

Research consistently shows that visuals don't just decorate – they reinforce. Adding illustrations or graphics to content can improve memory retention by around 20%, and when paired with interactive reinforcement, the boost can reach 32% over text-only material. This is explained by the well-established Picture Superiority Effect: people are far more likely to recall information presented as images rather than words alone, because visuals are processed through both verbal and visual channels in the brain, embedding them more deeply in memory.

I follow three rules when creating slides and visuals for my presentations:

- One idea per slide.
- Contrast and clarity.
- Metaphorical visuals.

Thanks to Generative AI it has become incredibly easy for even someone like me without a designers eye to create impactful and memorable images and videos to explain my ideas.

Words make them listen. Visuals make them remember.

Step 7: Rehearse Like a Performer

Even if you're "just" presenting at a quarterly review, rehearse like it matters – because it does.

I test beats and transitions. I play with pauses and tempo. I record myself and watch for where the energy dips. Now I also run those videos through AI tools. They flag details I might miss – suggesting I hold a pause a beat longer after a big line, or adjust how I use my hands to give a point more weight.

Years ago, in one of the first episodes of the SuperCreativity podcast, I interviewed Tom Jackson, Taylor Swift's performance coach. He told me how they rehearsed every detail: exactly where she should stand before hitting the high note, how to move across the stage to build authority, how to project charisma under the lights. What once was the preserve of superstars is now accessible to anyone. With a camera and an AI performance coach, you can rehearse like a professional – and become a sharper speaker, communicator, and leader.

Step 8: Deliver with Connection, Not Perfection

On the day, remember the essentials:

- **Connect first.**
- **Serve, don't impress.**
- **Make the audience the hero – you're the guide.**

Artificial Intelligence can prepare your material. But only your conviction can persuade in the moment.

As Sir Jonathan Ive once said, "We believe that technology is at its very best; at its most empowering when it disappears." That's the ideal. Your tech – the slides, the AI tools – should fade so completely into the background that your presence, your message, and your emotional connection are all the audience remembers.

Step 9: Review, Refine, Repeat

Finally, close the loop. Ask for feedback. Watch the recording. Adjust for next time. Every persuasion moment is rehearsal for the next.

Think about elite athletes. Every match, every race, every play is recorded, broken down, and analysed. They study what worked, what slipped, and how to get better. Why shouldn't a C-suite executive or senior leader do the same?

Now AI makes that kind of analysis available to anyone. Upload your presentation and tools can track your pacing, tone, body language, even where attention rose or dipped. They'll flag details you might miss: a rushed transition, a moment where a pause could add power, a gesture that distracted instead of reinforced. Pair that precision with your own judgment and intuition, and each performance becomes sharper, more confident, more persuasive than the last.

From Presentation to Platform

The Taylor-Made Persuasion Loop isn't just a preparation checklist. It's a system for persuasion at scale.

Whether you're an executive pitching to the board, a manager seeking resources, or a leader addressing an all-hands meeting, this loop helps you:

- Understand your audience.
- Shape a narrative that lands.
- Deliver a message that moves people.

And it ensures your best ideas don't die in a slide deck. They take root, spread, and create change.

So the next time you face an important presentation – whether five colleagues in a conference room or five thousand on a livestream – remember:

Don't wing it. Taylor-Make it.

The Taylor-Made Persuasion Loop gives you the process – a step-by-step way to prepare, tailor, and deliver your most important messages with confidence. But even the best process needs fuel. And in persuasion, that fuel is story.

Stories are what transform facts into meaning. They're what turn a proposal into a possibility people can see themselves in. They're what make your audience not just understand your message, but feel it. In the next sub-chapter, we'll explore why storytelling is the ultimate delivery system for persuasion – and how to use it to make your ideas unforgettable.

STORYTELLING IS THE DELIVERY SYSTEM

"I've learned that people will forget what you said, people will forget what you did, but people will never forget how you made them feel." – Maya Angelou

Storytelling as the Delivery System
Facts inform. Stories transform.

A few years ago, researchers placed people in MRI scanners and asked them to listen to stories. What they found was remarkable: when someone tells a story, the same areas of the brain light up in the listener as in the storyteller. The audience doesn't just hear the story – they live it.

That's the power of narrative transportation. It pulls us out of the role of observer and into the role of participant. For leaders, this matters because numbers may capture attention in the moment, but stories create memory and meaning. People will forget last quarter's spreadsheet. But they won't forget the story of the customer whose life was changed by your product, the founder who refused to abandon an impossible idea, or the team that delivered the breakthrough when everyone else thought it couldn't be done.

And now, Human+Machine collaboration is opening new horizons for storytelling. Marketers, advertisers, and filmmakers are already using AI to turn concepts into polished stories in days instead of months – for a fraction of the cost and with teams a fraction of the size. A handful of creatives with the right tools can now storyboard, edit, score, and visualise a campaign that once required entire departments and seven-figure budgets. AI doesn't replace the storyteller's imagination; it accelerates the journey from idea to impact.

Frameworks like the 4Ps give persuasion its structure. But story gives it soul. And with Human+Machine collaboration, we now have the tools to tell those stories bigger, faster, and more powerfully than ever.

Why Stories Persuade

Stories work because they do what data alone cannot: they connect emotionally. Neuroscientists call this "neural coupling" – when a story activates the same patterns in the brain of the listener as in the speaker. A good story doesn't just land as information; it lands as experience.

For executives, this matters in every persuasion moment. At the quarterly review, the financials may fade, but the story of how a team turned around a failing division will endure. In a board pitch, charts blur together –but the story of a competitor's mistake, and the lesson it carries, will stick.

Stories as Contrast

Every persuasive story has contrast built in. Nancy Duarte calls it the "world as it is" versus the "world as it could be". Leaders persuade by naming the present reality, then opening a window into a better future.

This mirrors the 4P Framework:
- *Position* and *Problem* describe the world as it is.
- *Possibilities* and *Proposal* paint the world as it could be.

Without that tension, stories fall flat. With it, they create momentum.

Three Stories Every Persuader Needs

Every executive, founder, or speaker should have a small library of stories at their disposal – not memorised word for word, but ready to tell naturally.

The three foundations are:
- **Origin Story** – How you or your idea came to be.
  Shows credibility, passion, and purpose.
  "I remember visiting our production facility in Detroit when the idea first struck…"
- **Customer-as-Hero Story** – A person like your audience who succeeded using your solution, insight, or method.
  Shows relevance, results, and empathy.
  "Take Anika, a regional operations lead in Berlin, who…"
- **External Parallel Story** – A surprising or unrelated example that illustrates your point.
  Shows creativity, novelty, and strategic thinking.
  "In 2001, NASA faced a similar challenge…"

When I speak to AI leaders, I often tell stories about chefs, musicians, or even a 3D-printed cheesecake – because the metaphor unlocks insight. If your audience is stuck, sometimes the best move is to take them somewhere else first.

How to Find Your Stories

- **Look inward:** What personal or professional moment shaped your perspective?
- **Look outward:** What are your customers, clients, or competitors doing that others can learn from?
- **Look around:** What surprising thing happened last week that illustrates your message?

And remember: it's not about being cinematic. It's about being specific.

Don't say: "We faced challenges." Say: "It was 2:13 a.m. in the Jakarta office, and the VPN had gone down for the third time."

The detail is the hook. The emotion is the glue. The structure carries the message.

Storytelling Tips from the Stage

Want to turn a good story into a persuasive one? Use these pro-level techniques from years of stagecraft and speaking mentors:

- **Start late:** Drop us straight into the action. Skip the back-story.
  "I was already sweating by the time I reached the front desk."
- **Use sensory language:** Help the audience feel it.
  "The silence in the boardroom was louder than the rain outside."
- **Build loops:** Start a story, shift to another idea, then return to close the loop. Suspense creates rhythm.
- **Contrast tension and release:** Alternate between struggle and resolution.

"We thought it was over. Then we found a pattern in the data…"

- **Frame with meaning:** Don't just tell the story – tie it back to the bigger point.

"And that's when I realised: creativity isn't about thinking differently, it's about seeing what others missed."

What Makes a Story Persuasive?

1. **Relevance** – It mirrors your audience's world.
2. **Emotion** – It generates feeling, not just facts.
3. **Transformation** – It shows a before, a struggle, and an after.
4. **Believability** – It's honest. Ideally, a little vulnerable.
5. **Momentum** – It moves the audience closer to your idea.

Storytelling and AI? Yes, and…

You might wonder: can AI really help with storytelling?

Absolutely – as a draft partner, idea generator, or analytical tool.

- I use AI to suggest metaphors, test tone, or generate alternative endings.
- AI can analyse your script and show whether it appeals more to logic or emotion – and which type your audience values most.
- It can score stories for novelty, tension, or clarity.
- It can even generate quick **visuals or mock-ups** to help you illustrate an abstract idea.
- And it can mine other industries for parallels – surfacing how a hospital solved a logistics challenge, or how a sports team reshaped its culture – insights you can adapt to your own field.

But the soul of the story still comes from you.

The AI may give you a hundred options. Only you know which one has heart.

Closing: Lead with Story

At every level of leadership, persuasion is powered by story.

You can structure your message with the 4Ps. You can refine it with the Taylor-Made Persuasion Loop. But story is what brings it to life, creates belief, and makes your message travel.

Don't just explain the numbers. Tell the story of what they mean. That's how you move people – and that's how ideas take root.

SuperCollaborative Storytelling

Not long ago, a client of mine – a senior executive at a global manufacturing company – had to persuade the board to invest in AI for supply chain forecasting. She had the numbers: reduced costs, faster shipping times, higher reliability. But she knew the data alone wouldn't move them.

So she asked AI to help. First, it mined customer reviews and surfaced dozens of stories about delayed deliveries and frustrated clients. One stood out: a small retailer in Mexico City who lost a crucial holiday season because a shipment arrived two weeks late. The AI helped her craft that story into a short narrative, even suggesting metaphors that framed supply chains as the "circulatory system" of the company.

When she stood before the board, she didn't start with the cost savings slide. She began with the Mexico City story – the shopkeeper, the empty shelves, the customers who never came back. Only then did she show how AI could prevent it from happening again.

The result? The board approved the investment. Not because of the numbers alone, but because the story made them feel the stakes.

That's the power of Human+Machine collaboration in persuasion: data for the head, story for the heart, courage for the gut. And now, every leader has those tools within reach.

As the historian and writer Yuval Noah Harari reminds us: "Homo sapiens rule the world because we are the only animal that can cooperate flexibly in large numbers – and we do so because we believe in shared stories."

How could AI help you craft a story that not only persuades others of your idea, but wins their hearts and minds along the way?

THE FINAL ACT: WHO NEEDS CONVINCING?

"The most courageous act is still to think for yourself.
Aloud." – Coco Chanel

Speak as If the Future Depends on It

So let's bring this full circle.

If creativity is the spark of the idea, and collaboration is the flame, then persuasion is the wind that carries the idea.

It's the force that turns a private idea into a shared belief. A sketch on a napkin into a movement. A prototype into a product. A vision into something real.

Because having the idea isn't enough. Building the solution isn't enough. Even showing the results isn't enough.

You have to make people care. You have to make people believe. You have to persuade.

Whether you're in a boardroom securing funding, on Zoom rallying a cross-functional team, or on stage with 2,000 faces staring back at you – the final act of creativity is not the making. It's the convincing.

And here's the thing: this isn't just about being a better speaker or presenter. It's about being braver.

It's about standing up for your idea – especially when it's fragile, unfinished, or daring to challenge the status quo. It's about having the courage to risk a "no" in pursuit of a "yes".

And if that idea matters – if it can improve lives, grow teams, shift culture, spark innovation, or serve a bigger mission – then it deserves your full voice.

Beyond the Room

And in this age, you don't stand alone. SuperCollaboration, this idea of Human+Machine collaboration can elevate your voice. AI can help you shape your message, test it, refine it, and amplify it across audiences you may never meet in person.

A single presentation can now become a hundred touchpoints: a video, a blog, a personalised message for every department or market. What was once one room can now be the world. AI gives you scale. But only you can bring the conviction. Only you can make people believe.

So the next time you step back into the world of pitch decks, project plans, strategy reviews, campaign proposals, and investor meetings, ask yourself one simple but powerful question:

Who needs convincing?

Whose belief do you need to earn? Whose worldview do you need to challenge? Whose energy, budget, time, or endorsement do you need to move your idea forward?

That's your starting point.

Now use what you've learned. Use your 4Ps. Use your stories. Use your preparation. Use your humanity.

And then speak – with data in your head, conviction in your heart, and courage in your gut. Speak as if the future depends on it.

Because sometimes it does!

Persuasion is what shifts an idea from being yours alone to something others want to build with you. But persuasion is only the beginning. To make SuperCreativity a reality, you and your team need tools – techniques that turn possibility into practice, spark collaboration into results, and build a culture where creativity becomes the norm.

That's where we go next.

In Part 4, I'll open up the SuperCreator's toolbox: a set of proven methods you can apply both individually and with your team. These aren't abstract theories, but hands-on techniques designed to help you generate, shape, and deliver ideas – not just once, but again and again.

If the first three parts of this book have given you the concepts, theory and examples. Part 4 puts tools in your collective hands. Tools to help you and your colleagues think more creatively, collaborate more effectively, and embed SuperCreativity into the everyday rhythm of your work.

Because hopefully I've now convinced you that the future isn't built by lone geniuses. It's built by teams who know how to unlock their creativity – and put it into action.

Next Actions

Do This Week
1. **Identify your persuasion moment.** Choose one upcoming meeting, presentation, or conversation where your idea needs buy-in.
2. **Map your 4Ps.** Use the framework – Position, Problem, Possibilities, Proposal – to sketch your persuasive arc.
3. **Apply the Taylor-Made Method.** Profile your audience, design your message, choose your stories, and rehearse your delivery – blending AI's precision with your own creativity and conviction.
4. **Rehearse once more.** Record yourself, watch it back, and make one small change – a pause, a gesture, a tighter opening.

Download the worksheet for this chapter on Persuasion as well as bonus content at www.supercreativitybook.com

Reflect and Reframe

Questions to Ask Yourself
- Who really needs convincing for my idea to succeed – and am I giving them my best effort?
- What's one story I could tell that would help people *feel* the stakes, not just understand the facts?
- How could I use the Taylor-Made Method – audience insight, narrative design, and AI refinement – to sharpen my next persuasion moment?
- What would I attempt to persuade others of if I was willing to risk a "no" in pursuit of a bigger "yes"?

Key Takeaways

SuperCreator's Cheat Sheet
- Persuasion is not decoration – it's the second half of creativity, the bridge from imagination to impact.
- The 4P Framework (Position, Problem, Possibilities, Proposal) provides a universal structure for shaping persuasive messages.
- The Taylor-Made Method blends human empathy and creativity with AI's analytic power to design, refine, and deliver high-impact persuasion.
- Storytelling is the ultimate delivery system: it connects emotionally, builds momentum, and makes ideas unforgettable.
- The essential question for every creative leader: Who needs convincing?

PART 4

THE SUPERCREATOR'S TOOLBOX

CHAPTER 9

PRACTICAL TOOLS FOR CREATIVE LEADERS

"If the only tool you have is a hammer, you tend to see every problem as a nail." – Abraham Maslow

The SuperCreativity Toolbox

Each year, I deliver dozens of keynotes and workshops across more than 25 countries, speaking to audiences that range from C-suite executives and board members to frontline teams in sales, strategy, HR, finance, operations, and marketing. Across industries – from banking and engineering to healthcare and fashion – one truth remains constant: everyone wants more innovative ideas, but few have a proven system for making those ideas happen.

Recently a middle manager from one of the world's largest soft drinks companies approached me after a keynote in Austin, Texas. She shared a recent situation where her boss came up to her with a supply-chain problem and told her to, "Just go away and come up with some creative ideas". She was being asked to "be creative" without being provided with any frameworks, training or resources. She felt frustrated and undervalued. She lacked some basic creative thinking tools to help her "be creative".

That's what this section of the book is about. It's your SuperCreator's Toolbox: a collection of simple but powerful tools to help you and your team generate, develop, and evaluate ideas more effectively. Whether your goal is to launch a new product, cut costs, improve customer experience, or pitch a bold strategy to sceptical stakeholders, these tools will give you the frameworks and language to think and act more creatively. They're designed not only to help you think differently, but to help others around you do the same.

We're moving beyond creativity theory now. This is application. This is practice. This is where creative instincts become repeatable results.

Why Tools Matter

When it comes to producing and shaping new ideas – whether individually or with a team – you really only have five options:
1. **Reason:** Research and try to logic your way to an idea.
2. **Borrow:** Adapt or adopt an idea from someone else (perhaps a competitor).
3. **Wait:** Hope for inspiration to strike. Good luck with that.
4. **Outsource:** Hire a consultant to do the thinking for you (and they will charge you handsomely for doing so).
5. **Apply tools:** Use a deliberate set of creative methods to generate ideas on demand.

It's this final approach we'll focus on. The tools I'm about to share have been refined over hundreds of workshops, thousands of brainstorming sessions, and millions of Post-it notes.
Here's why they work:

- They're simple and easy to remember.
- They create a shared language across teams.
- They work with – not against – our cognitive biases.
- They help you avoid "the intelligence trap".
- They generate hypotheses you can test and refine.
- They can be adapted to any stage of the creative process.

Let's dive in.

TOOL 1: CURIOUS QUESTIONS

Peter Drucker once said, "The most common source of mistakes in management decisions is the emphasis on finding the right answer rather than the right question."

Too often, we rush toward solutions without asking whether we're solving the right problem. Curious Questions is a simple, team-based tool designed to disrupt that reflex and surface insights you didn't know you needed.

How It Works

Step 1: Define the Challenge or Opportunity

In a small group, each person identifies a real challenge or opportunity they care about. The group then chooses one to focus on.

Step 2: Generate Questions Only

Everyone in the group – except the person whose challenge or opportunity it is – asks a stream of questions. Questions, questions, questions and only questions. The person whose challenge or opportunity it is stays quiet and simply writes down the myriad of questions that the others generate. The goal is quantity here. If you give your team 10 minutes for this task then each member of the group should generate at least 10 questions. Examples include:

- What if we inverted the problem?
- Who else has solved this?
- What does success actually look like?
- How might we solve this problem with half the budget?
- When would this solution matter most – and when might it fail?
- What assumptions are we making that could be wrong?
- Why does it matter?
- Who needs to be convinced of the importance of this challenge or opportunity?
- What would this look like if it were easy?

Encourage playful, contrarian, and even "impossible" questions. Often, the outliers spark the most valuable insights.

Step 3: Reflect and Select

The challenge-owner reviews the list and asks:

- "Which of these questions, if answered, would create the biggest opportunity to disrupt the status quo?"
- "Which of these questions, if solved, would make many of the others irrelevant?"

The questions that stand out become prompts for deeper research, experimentation, or strategic reframing.

Case Example

In a workshop with a global pharmaceutical company, one group explored the challenge: "How do we improve patient adherence to medication?"

A curious question emerged: "What if we made it impossible for patients to take the medication?" That single question sparked the development of a smart blister pack prototype that increased adherence by 23% in trials.

Use It When
- You're stuck or facing a fuzzy challenge.
- You need fresh ways of seeing a familiar problem.
- You want to encourage catalytic questioning rather than quick fixes.

TOOL 2: RANDOM WORDS

Not all great ideas come from linear thinking. Some of the most original breakthroughs happen when we step sideways, disrupt our expectations, and make unusual associations. That's the logic behind the random words tool – a simple method for provoking surprising connections and unlocking dormant creativity.

How It Works
Choose a random word (flip open a random page in a book or dictionary, or even ask an AI to generate a random word). Then challenge yourself or your team to connect that word to your current problem or opportunity. Ask questions such as:
- "What if our service worked like this object?"
- "What does this word inspire us to change about the customer experience?"
- "How can we apply the characteristics (e.g. soft, metallic, squishy) of this word or object to our problem?
- "How might this word suggest an entirely new business model?"

AI can also take this further: instead of one random word, it can instantly generate dozens of prompts drawn from different industries, cultures, or metaphors. Suddenly, your team isn't just working with magnet – you're exploring orchard, compass, or water – each one pushing your imagination in unexpected directions.

Creative Roots

Romanian-born writer and Nobel Laureate Herta Müller used a version of this technique to cope with censorship and trauma. She cut words from magazines and rearranged them into poetic collages that broke through narrative and emotional blocks. The unexpected juxtapositions opened new insights.

Rock legend David Bowie did something similar with artist Brian Eno, using the "cut up" method: scattering words from newspapers or lyrics across a page, then reassembling them into surreal new compositions. Bowie described the result as "a complete haphazard set of juxtapositions" – sparks that fuelled some of his most visionary songs.

Team Application

In a European fintech company, a design sprint had stalled on clichéd user interface ideas. A randomly drawn word – magnet – sparked a breakthrough. One designer imagined an interface that would "pull users toward their financial goals". That insight led to a drag-and-drop feature where customers could visually reallocate funds, making goal-setting intuitive and engaging.

Use It When
- Your team is stuck in conventional thinking.

- You're facing creative block.
- You need inspiration from outside your domain.
- You want to bring AI in as a "metaphor machine" – generating unusual associations you might never consider on your own.

TOOL 3: OUT (rageous Statements)

How It Works

Start with an outrageous, deliberately provocative statement. For example:

- "What if our product was free?"
- "What if we fired all our managers?"
- "What if customers designed every product?"
- "What if we closed all our physical stores?"
- "What if employees set their own salaries?"
- "What if our most profitable business line disappeared tomorrow?"
- "What if our brand had to grow without advertising?"
- "What if AI ran the company?"
- "What if we only worked four hours a week?"
- "What if competitors marketed our products for us?"
- "What if regulators wrote our next strategy?"

At first, some of these may sound absurd. That's the point. The value of these OUT(rageous) Statements or "What if" Questions isn't because you'll ever literally do these things. It's that they jolt you out of a fixed way of thinking about your problem, opportunity, product, service, or business model. They force you to loosen rigid assumptions and consider new angles.

What I've seen time and again in workshops is that, during the discussion of the outrageous idea, someone proposes a variation that is possible – and valuable. OUT acts as a bridge: from a fixed mindset to a more flexible, fluid, and creative one.

Example

One client wanted to grow furniture sales but without opening more stores – a classic growth dilemma. To jolt the team out of conventional thinking, we posed an OUT statement: "What if our customers were our salespeople?"

At first, the idea sounded far-fetched. After all, customers aren't trained to sell, and sales traditionally requires showrooms, staff, and infrastructure. But the provocation sparked debate: What would it look like if customers could share their love of the products directly with others? What if their enthusiasm could become the sales channel?

That line of questioning opened up new possibilities. The team began exploring how they might harness social proof and peer influence. Soon, the conversation shifted: If customers are already showing their furniture to friends and family when they visit, how could we turn those moments into opportunities to buy?

The breakthrough came with the idea of adding QR codes to customers" furniture. When friends or family visited this customers home and admired their new coffee table, the visitor could simply scan the code, browse the product details, and place an order on the spot. The host would earn a commission on any purchase – effectively turning loyal customers into brand advocates and creating a new peer-to-peer retail channel.

What began as an outrageous OUT statement – What if our

customers were our salespeople?" – ended in a practical innovation with real business value. That's the essence of OUT: using provocation as a bridge from fixed assumptions to flexible, high-potential solutions.

Case Study

At a major automotive company's leadership retreat, one team worked with the statement: "What if we gave away our new product for free?"

The provocation sparked the design of a freemium model for fleet management software, capturing new market segments and generating revenue through analytics subscriptions.

The Human+Machine Twist

Traditionally, facilitators or leaders would generate a handful of OUT statements. Today, AI can act as a partner – instantly generating dozens of "What if?" scenarios across industries, geographies, or customer segments.

Feed your challenge into an AI tool and ask: "Give me 20 outrageous ideas for this problem." You'll get everything from "What if we replaced our CEO with an AI?" to "What if your hospital operated like Netflix?" Most will be impractical. That's fine. The value lies in how they spark debate, laughter, and new pathways of thought.

AI provides the raw provocation; humans provide the judgment to spot the seed of something feasible – and potentially transformative.

Use It When

- You need to break free from default assumptions.

- A team is stuck in incremental ideas.
- You want to encourage risk-taking and "what if" thinking.
- You need a bridge from fixed mindsets to more open, fluid possibilities.

TOOL 4: PNC (Positive, Negative, Curious)

This deceptively simple framework is a game-changer for evaluating ideas collaboratively and constructively – especially in teams with strong opinions.

How It Works

When reviewing a proposal, ask three questions:
- What's Positive about this idea?
- What's Negative about it?
- What's Curious or interesting about it? (i.e. neither positive or negative)

The structure creates psychological safety by giving space for critique without confrontation. It invites nuance, balances optimism with realism, and encourages people to reflect before they react.

Why It Matters for Leaders

If you're a leader or manager, PNC isn't just a tool for group dialogue – it can develop your own creativity. Even if you secretly think a colleague's idea is the "dumbest thing you've ever heard" running through a PNC forces you to explore it from different angles. Often, that process sparks new connections or reveals value you hadn't seen before.

Industry Use

In a workshop with a multinational retail chain, leaders were debating whether to reduce store hours. Many opposed the idea outright. But when the group applied PNC, the "Curious" angle opened up a fresh line of thought: What if AI could predict customer footfall and dynamically adjust store hours?

Everyday Use

PNC also works beyond the workplace. Try it next time your child asks for more pocket money:

- **Positive:** "I can buy more sweets."
- **Negative:** "I might lose all my teeth."
- **Curious:** "What if I gave some of it to charity instead?"

By reframing even simple requests, PNC encourages more creative thinking and richer conversations.

Use It When

- You need to evaluate ideas without shutting them down too early.
- Discussions risk becoming confrontational or polarised.
- You want to build a culture where critique is constructive and curiosity is valued.
- You want to spark creativity in yourself by exploring perspectives you might otherwise dismiss.

TOOL 5: THE VIRTUAL ADVISORY BOARD

This tool uses the power of simulation and generative AI to pressure-test your idea before you ever pitch it. But its value goes deeper. It helps you challenge your cognitive biases, sharpen your communication, and radically improve your chances of persuading others.

Our Brain's Shortcut System

Your creative brain consumes enormous amounts of energy every day. To conserve effort, it relies on heuristics – mental shortcuts or "rules of thumb".

You see a problem, and your brain responds: "I've seen this before. Here's the answer."

That works… until it doesn't.

Shortcuts often lead to what psychologists call cognitive biases. There are more than 50 identified types, including:

- **Confirmation Bias:** Seeking out information that confirms what we already believe.
- **Anchoring Bias:** Relying too heavily on the first piece of information we hear.
- **Authority Bias:** Deferring to perceived experts, even when they may be wrong.
- **Groupthink:** Avoiding dissent to preserve harmony.

Generative AI can help you step outside these ruts. It lets you adopt other perspectives – those of your boss, your client, your board – and simulate how your idea might be received. By preparing for resistance before it arises, you dramatically improve your odds of success.

How It Works

1. **Assemble your board.** List five or six people you respect. They can be living or deceased, fictional or real, famous or personal mentors. These become your **Virtual Advisory Board**.

2. **Run the simulation.** Head to your AI tool of choice and simulate a conversation with each advisor. Ask them:

   » "What would you challenge about this idea?"

   » "What risks do you see that I might be blind to?"

   » "How would you position this idea to a sceptical executive?"

3. **Analyse the feedback.** Look for common threads, unexpected objections, or fresh angles that sharpen your case.

Your Turn

Think about a creative project you're working on – or one you've been putting off. Write down five or six names you'd want on your Virtual Advisory Board. Then simulate their feedback. Remember: they're advisors, not deciders. They challenge you, but the final judgment is still yours.

Use It When

- You're refining an idea before presenting it.
- You're preparing to persuade stakeholders.
- You want to uncover blind spots in your own thinking.

TOOL 6: VOD (Variations, Options, Decisions)

Why It Matters

In fast-paced environments, it's tempting to grab the first good idea and run with it. But innovative teams know that quantity breeds quality. VOD is a structured tool that forces you to widen the lens, explore multiple angles, and only then narrow down to a decision.

It's especially powerful when you're navigating uncertainty, balancing stakeholder demands, or managing competing constraints. VOD gives you a disciplined way to expand your thinking – and then converge on the best path.

How It Works
1. **Variations**
   Start by identifying different ways of framing the problem or solution – think of these as alternate realities.
   - Launching a product? Variations might include a subscription model, a one-time purchase, or a freemium version.
2. **Options**
   For each variation, brainstorm multiple options – specific execution paths.
   - For the subscription model, options might include monthly vs. annual plans, bundling with other services, or offering a trial period.
3. **Decisions**
   Evaluate your options across variations. What stands out in terms of feasibility, alignment with customer needs, or strategic fit? Pick the best direction for now – and capture your reasoning so you can revisit later.

Facilitator Tip
Use a large whiteboard or digital workspace. Create three columns: Variations, Options, Decisions. Ask team members to populate them with sticky notes or digital cards. Then step back, look for patterns, and discuss which direction has the strongest potential. You can also use this tool to mindmap your ideas and see random connections and possible combinations.

Use Cases

A North American consumer goods company wanted to reduce packaging waste without affecting shelf life. Using VOD, they explored three variations: fully compostable packaging, reusable packaging, and packaging-as-a-service.

An HR department in a technology company used VOD to redesign onboarding. Variations included live workshops, self-paced courses, and gamified experiences. Within each, they generated multiple options for format and delivery.

Use It When

- You're facing complex, multi-faceted decisions.
- Stakeholders have competing priorities.
- Early convergence would risk shutting down innovation too soon.

TOOL 7: GLF (Gain, Logic, Fear)

GLF is a simple but powerful tool for crafting messages that persuade others of your idea. It ensures your pitch resonates on three levels: aspiration, reason, and risk.

How It Works

When presenting an idea, make sure you can clearly articulate:
- **Gain** – What benefit does this idea offer?
- **Logic** – What rational argument supports it?
- **Fear** – What risk do we avoid by taking this path?

By weaving together all three, you create a balanced message that appeals to both the head and the heart.

Application

In a healthcare innovation pitch, one team proposed virtual post-op checkups:

- **Gain:** Faster recovery times and higher patient satisfaction.
- **Logic:** 42% of complications occur within the first 72 hours after surgery.
- **Fear:** Missed warning signs can lead to fatalities – and lawsuits.

Using GLF, the team secured funding from conservative stakeholders who might otherwise have resisted.

Use Case

A chemicals company in Africa was debating whether to invest in creating digital twins of all their production facilities. The scale and cost made some leaders hesitant. Framing the proposal through GLF helped clarify the value:

- **Gain:** Digital twins would enable predictive maintenance, reduce downtime, and improve overall efficiency – boosting production output and profitability.
- **Logic:** Studies showed that companies using digital twins cut unplanned outages by up to 30% and improved asset lifespans significantly.
- **Fear:** Without digital twins, the company risked costly breakdowns, safety incidents, and losing ground to international competitors already adopting this technology.

By structuring the case around Gain, Logic, and Fear, the leadership team aligned around the investment and approved a phased rollout.

Use It When

- You're pitching ideas to leadership or sceptical teams.
- You need to frame a proposal for both opportunity and risk.
- You want to make your argument compelling across emotional and rational dimensions.

TOOL 8: FUTURE PACING

Purpose

Future Pacing is designed to stretch your thinking across multiple time horizons. It helps leaders and teams move beyond short-term fixes and anticipate long-term consequences and opportunities.

How It Works

Ask: "What would happen if we implemented this idea in…"
- **3 months**
- **1 year**
- **1–5 years**
- **5–10 years**
- **10+ years**

By deliberately scanning different horizons, you reveal risks, dependencies, and opportunities that may not be visible in the immediate term.

Example

An online retailer applied Future Pacing to drone deliveries.
- **3 months:** Immediate regulatory and safety issues domi-

nated the discussion.

- **1 year:** Pilot programs with limited customer adoption were realistic.
- **5 years:** Entirely new opportunities emerged – securing ownership of key airspace corridors and building partnerships with municipal governments.

That long-term foresight positioned the company ahead of competitors who were still focused only on the regulatory barriers.

Use It When

- Long-term strategic alignment matters.
- You want to surface second- and third-order effects of an idea.
- You need to prepare stakeholders for both near-term action and future possibilities.

Download the worksheet for this chapter on Tools as well as bonus content at www.supercreativitybook.com

CONCLUSION

*"Twenty years on from now you will be more disappointed
by the things you didn't do than by the things you did do.
So throw off the bowlines. Sail away from the safe
harbor. Catch the trade winds in your sails.
Explore, dream, discover."* – Mark Twain

The Age of SuperCreativity

We've reached the end of this book, but perhaps the real journey is just beginning.

You've explored the myths that hold us back – of the lone genius, the creative type, and the mistaken belief that creativity is a kind of magic reserved for a select few. You've discovered the truths that liberate us: that creativity is collaborative, that you were born creative, and that creativity can be developed and refined.

You've walked through the Eight Ps of SuperCreativity – Purpose, Personality, Practice, People, Process, Place, Product, and Persuasion – each one a lens to see, develop, and amplify your creative potential. You've met SuperCreatives in every industry, from chefs and scientists to designers and data analysts. And you've explored what it looks like to collaborate not only with humans, but also with artificial intelligence.

In doing so, you've unlocked something powerful: the understanding that the future isn't waiting to be discovered. It's waiting to be designed.

We are entering an era where creativity is no longer optional. It's a necessity.

Not just for artists and entrepreneurs, but for managers, marketers, and technologists. For anyone navigating complexity, change, or challenge. Creativity lets us see the world not only as it is – but as it could be. And SuperCreativity gives us the tools to build that world, faster and more effectively, with the help of exponential technologies like artificial intelligence.

But tools alone are not enough.

Technology like AI can accelerate the creative process. It can help us generate more ideas, test more options, and scale more quickly. But the real innovation lies in how we choose to use these tools. The real breakthrough is in the questions we ask, the values we embed, the purpose that drives us.

Because ultimately, creativity is not about novelty. It's about meaning.

It's about solving the right problems (and searching for new ones to solve). About building products that serve human needs, stories that move people to action, and systems that reflect our highest values – not just our latest algorithms.

SuperCreativity begins not in the software, but in the self.

It begins with your decision to show up differently – to lead with curiosity, to embrace collaboration, to engage in courageous acts of creation even when the outcome is uncertain.

That's why this book hasn't just been about creativity in the abstract. It's been about action.

- Action in the face of uncertainty.
- Action despite the fear of failure.
- Action that turns ideas into impact.

Because the greatest threat to creativity today isn't a lack of ideas. It's inertia. It's imposter syndrome. It's the hesitation to act. It's the quiet voice that says, "Who am I to create something new?" when the better question is, "Who am I not to?"

You are not alone in this.

You are part of a growing global movement – of leaders, learners, builders, and dreamers who choose to see the world not as fixed, but as flexible. Not as predetermined, but as designable. These are the SuperCreatives. And now, you are one of them.

Let's be clear: SuperCreativity isn't a label. It's a practice. A way of thinking. A way of working. A way of being in the world. It's not about having all the answers. It's about being brave enough to continually ask better questions.

So, as you step back into your work and your life, ask yourself:

- What problem is calling out for a more creative solution?
- What conversation is waiting to be had?
- What idea have you been sitting on for too long?
- What future do you want to help build?
- And perhaps most powerfully: **Who needs convincing?**

Because that's the final act of creativity. Not just to imagine and build but to persuade. To help others see what you see, feel what you feel, and believe in the possibility of something better. To inspire the yes that turns ideas into reality.

You've learned how to do that. You've learned how to structure persuasive stories, how to tailor your message for impact, how to lead people not with pressure, but with purpose. You now have the mindset, the language, the tools, and the confidence to make a real difference.

But knowledge only becomes power when it's put into motion.

So here's my final challenge to you:

Pick one idea from this book – just one – and put it into practice this week. Use a creative tool with your team. Frame your next pitch using the 4P Framework. Reimagine how your team collaborates with AI. Ask a better question. Start a new habit. Build a prototype. Tell a story that matters.

Whatever it is, do something with it.

Because action is where creativity becomes transformation.

And as you do, remember this:

You don't have to do it alone. The age of the lone genius is over. The era of SuperCreativity has begun. Also like most things in life it's more fun doing it with others.

In this era, the most powerful innovations will come from those who collaborate deeply – with people and machines.

And the most important work you will do?

It won't just be the things you build.

It will be the lives you touch. The minds you open. The futures you help make possible.

The future is not written. It's designed. By people like you.

Now go create it.

APPENDIX

WHAT SHOULD I DO NEXT

Bonus Resources (Download)

Now that you understand the concept of SuperCreativity, it's time to put it into action in your life and work. Visit www.SuperCreativityBook.com to start augmenting and amplifying your own creativity by accessing the free worksheets that accompany this book.

Listen to the SuperCreativity Podcast (Podcast)

Keep your ideas flowing by joining James each week on the SuperCreativity Podcast. Hear from world-leading thinkers, authors, and innovators exploring what it means to be human in the age of artificial intelligence. Listen now at www.jamestaylor.me/podcast-episodes/

Watch the SuperCreativity TV Series (Vlog)

Go behind the scenes as James travels the world exploring creativity, innovation, and technology. Watch short, insightful videos that bring the ideas of SuperCreativity to life. Start watching at www.jamestaylor.me/blog

Invite James to Speak at Your Next Event (Keynotes)

Inspire your audience to embrace the future of creativity and human–AI collaboration. James Taylor delivers keynote speeches that educate, entertain, and energise audiences across the globe. Find out more at www.jamestaylor.me/speaking.

Bring SuperCreativity to Your Team (Workshops)

Transform inspiration into action through hands-on, interactive learning experiences. James's workshops help teams unlock innovative thinking, solve problems creatively, and apply Super-Creativity principles to real-world challenges. Learn more at www.jamestaylor.me/corporate-workshops

Access the Free Creative Process Course (Courses)

Unlock your creative potential with The Creativity Blueprint — a free, three-part video training series. Discover how to break through creative blocks, generate ideas effortlessly, and unleash your creative genius in five simple steps. Access the training at training.jamestaylor.me

Bring James in to Advise Your Board (Advisory)

Gain a strategic advantage at the intersection of human creativity and artificial intelligence. James advises boards on building creative cultures, accelerating innovation, leveraging artificial intelligence responsibly, and preparing their organisations for the future. Enquire at enquiries@jamestaylor.me

ACKNOWLEDGMENTS

We create in context. All creative work is shaped by the environment, culture, and circumstances in which it occurs. This book is truly a collaborative effort and would not have been possible without a small army of advisers, mentors, and creative minds. *SuperCreativity* is the culmination of eight years of research and the process of developing and delivering these ideas at hundreds of keynotes and workshops. In addition to the feedback from thousands of audience members, there are a few individuals I would like to acknowledge for their help.

Once I had formed the ideas in this book, it was the advice of my friends David Avrin, Maria Franzoni, Ron Kaufman, Elaine Pofeldt, and Joseph Alexander that helped me turn them into physical form. Thanks also to those who read early versions of the manuscript and provided invaluable feedback, including Anna Deppi, Maria Torres, Patrick Rooney, Philippe Arnauts, Robin Hoj, and Sabine Volckaert. Working with my copyeditor, Barry Lyons—whose humour and expertise were exactly what this first-time author needed—was a joy.

Next, I'd like to acknowledge my team, including Dodi Verzano and Annie Walls, for providing the support that allowed me to step back from speaking to focus on writing this book. Thanks also to the hundreds of guests who have appeared on my *SuperCreativity* podcast and summits, from whom I have learned so much about creativity, collaboration, and writing. In particular: Fredrik Haren, Amy Edmondson, Seth Godin, Ryan Holiday, Daniel Pink, Michael Bungay Stanier, Josh Linkner, Rita McGrath, Marcus du Sautoy, Roger Kneebone, Jay Papasan, David Allen, Phil M. Jones, Hal Gregersen, Donald Miller, James Schramko, Rutger Bregman, and Jack Canfield.

Speaking of speaking, I also want to thank the speaker bureau owners and agents who have been my champions and cheerleaders over the years. In particular: Richard, Angela, Peyton, and Carson Schelp of Executive Speakers Bureau (USA); Barrett Cordero, Craig Sherman, Amy Dernus, and Amy Eddy of BigSpeak (USA); Tom Kenyon-Slaney, Tatjana Marinko Teo, Katie Lo, Alexis Leseigneur, Meenal Nath, Bindu Malik Krishna, Rebecca Smale, Mariam Gonzales, and the London Speaker Bureau team (UK); Saana Azzam, Floyd Gabasa, Arsalan Iqbal, Abdulghafour Alsamman, and Anuj Antony of MENA Speakers (UAE); Cosimo Turroturro of Speakers Associates (UK); Leanne Christie, Shannon Briggs, and Jane Rowland Smith of Ovations (Australia); Andrew Vine of The Insight Bureau (Singapore); Priscilla Chan of Speakers Connect (Hong Kong); James Maroney and Francisco Rodriguez of SmartSpeakers (Mexico); Canada Stefl, Laurie Iverson, and Wendy Hirdler of Key Speakers (USA); Dan Risner of Leading Authorities (UK); Derek Sweeney and Danielle Sweeney of The Sweeney Agency (Canada); Melissa Mann of SpeakInc (USA); Kim King of Limelight Group (Canada); Gautam Ganglani, Ram Ganglani, and Rinkesh Patlekar of Right Selection (India); Mark Matthews of Champions Speakers (UK); Theresa Beenken and Hal Eckensweiler of National Speakers Bureau (Canada); and Simon Benedict Myatt Trenholm of Thinking Heads (USA).

I was fortunate to be raised in a home that valued creativity, and for this I must thank my parents, Martin Taylor and Elizabeth Taylor. To create is to remember where you came from.

Finally, I must thank my wife, Alison (Burns) - jazz singer, lawyer, engineer, actor, animal rights campaigner, and the finest creative collaborator and life partner one could wish for. The chapter on "Creative Pairs" is dedicated to you. You give me the grand inner life to accompany our grand outer life.